AUTUMN LEAVES

Aging, With and Without Dementia

SER Publishing
Reno, NV

Autumn Leaves
Aging, With and Without Dementia

Copyright © 2009 Steven Rubin, M.D.

10-Digit ISBN: 0-9774172-1-2
13-Digit ISBN: 978-0-9774172-1-6

Interior design and production by R.L. Rivers

DEDICATION

I affectionately dedicate this book,
To my wife, Julia,
For giving me the greatest gift,
Of time.

More than all that you guard,
guard your mind, for it is the source of life.
—Proverbs 4:23

Only a wise child can understand
the language of flowers and trees.
—Helen Keller

TABLE OF CONTENTS

PROLOGUE

My purpose in writing this book is to share what I see, know, and do as a psychiatric physician specializing in geriatric care. I am concerned about the accuracy of diagnosing older patients. I am concerned about appropriately medicating seniors. With so much new knowledge available about aging and cognitive declines, I believe that practical information and common sense result in optimal health-care delivery.

Rather than a medical text, this book is based on actual clinical experiences. It's meant to complement existing medical knowledge, reinforce good health, and stimulate creative living into late adulthood. This book takes a unique approach for understanding the effects of aging on brain function. It will help you see why dementia and cognitive declines occur, how to assess them, and what we can do to modify their courses. In addition, after reading this book you might look at trees and their leaves with a different perspective.

Through my studies of biology and the practice of psychiatric medicine, I have become aware of how much we stand to learn about brain function and dementia by observing the plant kingdom. Down to a single cell, trees and plants represent the biological blueprint of life, from which all higher forms originate. Plants were the first to have circulation, respiration, metabolism, reproduction, feelings, and responses. Trees can show us how to live, grow old, and die.

I start by illustrating this correlation by referring, from a historical perspective, to one of our oldest recorded texts, written thousands of years ago in an effort to communicate to succeeding generations how and why life exists as it does. I then address issues of cognitive declines and dementia and their effects on mood and behavior (known as "co-morbidities").

The second part of the book focuses on recognizing, understanding, and managing issues involved with aging, with and without dementia. This section is a call to action for navigating our own maturation process and improving our qualities of life as time inevitably passes. By first acting to preserve ourselves, we can best meet the needs of patients and loved ones experiencing cognitive declines, as discussed in the last chapters regarding assessment and intervention.

Tens of millions of people around the world are entering their later years. For most of them it is a beautiful season, a time for harvest and golden foliage, for readiness and integration, and for a different kind of happiness. Autumn leaves, and winter follows.

PART ONE

FALLING LEAVES

Chapter One

THE GENESIS AND EXODUS OF LIFE, DEATH, AND DEMENTIA

"Development is a continuous process that begins when an oocyte (ovum) is fertilized by a spermatozoon (sperm) and ends at death."
—Keith L. Moore, *The Developing Human*

"And God said: 'Let there be light.'"

From the Beginning

One of the earliest explanations of the creation of life, human life in particular, and how our evolved brains came to be is found in the Old Testament, Genesis, first chapter, page one. The following isn't a religious tract or a discussion of theology or the Bible. It's simply a medical reference to an ancient explanation of life that remains applicable today—all these millennia later.

It is written that on the first day, from the great watery void,

God created the world, giving it light and the energy of life.

On the second day, God separated the heavens and sky from the Earth. Air, percolating amongst the primordial elements, can now sustain life.

On the third day of creation, God separated land from water. The three states of matter—solid, liquid, and gas—were now differentiated. Together, the first carbon, oxygen, and hydrogen atoms became the first sugars, proteins, and fats, the building blocks of biology. The inert was now animated.

Also on the third day, the grasses, seed-bearing herbs, and fruit-bearing trees were created. From a mixture of sunlight, water, and the elements in the air and soil, the plant kingdom was established. Plants are the original models for cell life; their inner workings reproduce and assemble to form organisms. The tubular channels of plants between their roots and leaves represent the first circulatory systems. Their primitive biochemical nerve complexes sense and react to stimuli, such as touch, sunlight, and temperature changes. All life will come from the plant kingdom and depend on it for food and oxygen.

On the fourth day, God created cycles, separating the sun from the moon and stars and establishing the rhythm of days and nights that become seasons and years. Time and life are now in perpetual motion. The sun rises and sets. The winds and oceans ebb and flow. Flowers open and close; seeds are produced, germinated, and sewn. Leaves sprout in springtime and die in autumn. Everything breathes.

The fourth day of creation describes metabolism, the continuous conversion of mass into energy and energy back into mass. Biological substances are built, broken, and rebuilt again and again, as energy goes organic. Birth, reproduction, and death occur with the movement of time.

At the close of the fourth day, life flowed with activity. Respiration, consumption, reproduction, along with a rudimentary nervous system of stimuli—response, territoriality even—all existed in the plant world.

On the fifth day, it is written in the book of Genesis, God put fish in the water and birds in the sky. Tubes with appendages move about.

These mobile life forms now have a distinct nervous system. Primitive multi-cellular living things, which still exist in the ocean today, possessed web-like nerve nets. These early animals developed nerve cords; the cords grew bulges of nerves called neural lobes.

Brain stems were formed atop spinal cords, out of which cranial nerves evolved for the special senses. Eyes could see, ears could hear. This reptilian brain is the core nervous system of all mammals, a vital base beneath our highly evolved primate and human brain. The future of mankind has swum in and crawled out of the ocean and onto land, not just to alight and perch in the trees, but to eat, climb, and swing from them.

God, an ancient scribe wrote, began the sixth and final day by creating "every kind of living creature: cattle, creeping things, and wild beasts of every kind." Mammals possess a middle brain, a secondary level of centralized nerves that grows around and encases the primitive reptilian brain. Within this middle brain are the nerve centers and tracts that give us animals more exquisite senses and greater communication, along with more complex memory and judgment abilities. Motor dexterity is fine-tuned. To promote existence, mating and rearing behaviors, along with procuring food, shelter, and safety from predators, is much more sophisticated. So is pleasure.

The final act on the sixth day was the creation of man and

woman—humans, the highest cognitive-functioning animal of them all. We constitute the most evolved nervous system that nature (on this planet, anyway) has ever seen. The cerebral cortex is the crown of the tree that forms our central nervous system. Our primate brain gives us not just the deepest intellect, but also the widest range of emotion. We think, feel, move about, communicate, and behave dominantly. We understand the passage of time, of life and death. We have the most complicated capacities, second to nature, to control, kill, and heal.

As it was written thousands of years ago, we come from the light of the sun, the gases of the firmament, the fluids of the ocean, and the nutrients of the land. We come from the flora, birds, fish, reptiles, and the mammals of our previous selves. This is the genesis of our nervous system. We're modeled after the trees and vegetative life forms on which we rely for our survival. Our bodies mirror them microscopically and as a whole. Our modern nervous, digestive, and circulatory systems physically imitate the fundamental tubular organization seen in plants. We're made up of trunks, with arms and legs branching off, hair and nails growing from those.

The root of the cardiovascular system is the heart, the pump. The aorta is "king trunk," branching into such major vessels as the carotid arteries to the head, which branch into primary cerebral arteries in the brain, which divide into vascular networks of tree-like limbs of diminishing size.

Likewise, the human nervous system. The spine is our tap-root, from which large nerves branch outward, along with their assigned organs and appendages. Large nerve roots give rise to smaller ones, down the shoulder, arm, hand, and to the fingertips, until tiny hair-like nerves complete their two-way-communication links throughout the body. The human brain flowers at the top of the spinal tube, blossoming into a million branching nerves that mold into lobes and cortexes and end up shaped not unlike a cauliflower or a mighty oak tree.

Visualize the modern brain as a tree composed of nerve tracts running up and down the roots, trunk, and branches. At the end of the branches, each nerve cell in our mind is like a leaf whose job is to convert solid energy into electrical energy. The mind is alive as long as sparks of electrical energy are generated. The declines of aging may be delayed or slowed, but the brain cannot help but naturally lose brain cells.

Unlike leaves, new nerve cells don't grow annually, but memories, like falling leaves, can be replaced by new ones. Perhaps the best chance for realistically preventing dementia is by *using* the brain—keeping the synapses sparking and generating new buds of energy.

Any living system, be it a dandelion, an insect, or a single brain cell, can thrive only if its support system sustains it. Trees exposed to poor water, air, or soil suffer, as do people with breathing difficulties or who lack adequate nutrition. The branches and circulatory vessels farthest from the organism's core will be the first to be affected when sustenance is compromised.

The cells of the cerebral cortex, the most recently evolved of the entire central nervous system, are located farthest away from the core of the brain. This advanced region of the human mind is the most vulnerable to any occurrence of compromise. The cortex is the site of most cognitive losses, where the exodus of dementia often enters the picture.

The smallest nerves and blood vessels are like the shortest and thinnest branches of a tree: last to be serviced and first to lose life in times of shortages. Many dementias occur when the brain tissues farthest from the vascular trunks are service-impaired. Like the outermost part of a tree, when supplies run short, the outermost parts of the brain and nervous system throughout the body are the first to be sacrificed.

The onset of dementia can occur cell by cell, one leaf at a time, or from problems affecting the whole nerve tree. Stagnated circulation causes a slowing, then a stoppage, of the transfer of motion and energy at the molecular level. The edges start to lose vigor, integrity, and function. In the brain, the outer regions retract, compromising cognition and judgment. In distal regions, the cornucopia of memory withdraws.

As dementia progresses and the brain's network of nerve branches become pruned, we lose advanced human-intellect capabilities. Mammalian middle-brain functions become dominant, consistent with the symptoms of moderate-stage dementia.

As the mind recedes and dementia approaches its most advanced stages, what's left of the human brain function is not unlike that of a bird or a lizard. We're reduced to the most basic behaviors and instincts such as territoriality, feeding and elimination, and sleep. We exist. Our level of sentience becomes a question mark.

When vital organ functions fade, life ceases at the level of conscious thought, and our metabolism declines to the level of plants. When circulation approaches stagnation, living things proceed to die. They return to their elemental beginnings, no longer contained by walls and membranes. Like falling tree branches, the chains of sugar, protein, and fat molecules break apart until eventually an end is reached. The last leaf, if you will. Cells and their components are reduced again to hydrogen, oxygen, carbon, and nitrogen. There is no more differentiation among solid, liquid, and gas, no more separation of the waters from the land or firmament.

Finally, as it is written in the opening words of the Book of Genesis, on the seventh day, between the darkness and the light, there is rest. Life sleeps, awakens, and sleeps again, as it must.

Falling Leaves

Cognitive declines occur because everything that lives has to die.

The reasons our minds deteriorate are fundamentally similar to the vulnerabilities of trees and most other living organisms. We can understand dementia by considering all the assaults that a tree might fend off in order to survive: stress, disease, pestilence, natural and man-made toxins and traumas, and the genetic clock.

Look closely at a leaf from a tree. Every leaf of every tree is a world in itself, a universe, as is every cell of every person. Perhaps you're holding it by the stem (petiole), the pipeline of life between the leaf and the tree. The petiole is a system of tunnels, a channel from which smaller and smaller vessels branch throughout the leaf. Driven by energy from the sun, these vessels transport water and nutrition to and from the leaf. As long as it's in communication with the vascular system, every cell of every leaf gives and receives energy.

Similarly, people have arteries and veins, large and small, which circulate to and from all central body systems. When the tubular channels inside a man, woman, or plant become blocked or carry contents that are tainted or imbalanced, though the entire organism endures, it loses vitality. Notice how trees sometimes appear arthritic as they grow old and develop hardening of the arteries.

In time, leaves dry, their colors fade, and they fall. They appear to be at rest, but in fact, they're programmed to evolve in death by decomposing to their original elements. This returns the leaf and all life to the unformed, the void. As it was in the beginning.

Dementia, then, is like a deciduous tree with winter approaching. As the metaphoric leaves fall off the central nervous system and the brain's crown of integrity weakens, people sometimes lose their mental capacities. Memory cells fade and die.

But new buds mean new memories. As I explain and recommend throughout this book, our best chance for preserving cognitive function is by nourishing our roots, our limbs, and our hearts. In a later chapter I discuss how we can advance our health and life through a concept I call "gerolescence." What follows now is a discussion of cognitive declines and what happens to people who experience them.

Chapter Two

THE FOREST DEMENTIA

"Sans teeth, sans eyes, sans taste, sans everything."
—*As You Like It*

The word dementia comes from the Latin for "without mind." All of us begin life that way and it's how some of us will finish. Is dementia a blessing or a curse? Is it a state of helplessness and disorientation, or a time of having few responsibilities and for simply being in the moment?

Who suffers the most from dementia? To lose one's presence of mind is sometimes more difficult for everyone *except* the individual experiencing the loss.

Family and friends often relate how excruciating it is to observe, first-hand and powerless, the decline of a loved one. It can be heartbreaking to witness an intelligent and vivacious personality regress to that of a child or even an animal, eating with the hands or urinating on the floor. The spirit is vanquished, and we on the outside cannot revive it.

The person developing cognitive deficits may not even be aware of the decline. Oblivious to what they're going through, many dementia patients carry on complacently. The progression of dementia might sometimes be considered benevolent, providing release and relief from an overwhelming world of fear and struggle. Indeed, some welcome their cognitive winter, for they leave behind a life that had become empty or otherwise distressful. Happy is the child without a care.

In my career as a geriatric psychiatrist, I've encountered those who have graciously accepted their memory loss and responsibly relinquished their care into the hands of others. I have also known those who resisted going gently into that good night. Whether due to denial, fear, or pride, they complicate an already-frustrating situation. Perhaps the cruelest dementia situations occur when the afflicted are aware of, but powerless over, their own losses.

Although easier said than done, acceptance is perhaps the saving grace. Call it faith, conviction, courage, or dignity, acceptance means gratitude, accommodating reality, salvaging what remains, and facing one's own mortality.

Elders traditionally have the responsibility for leadership of those who will inevitably follow. By owning their attributes, they permit and encourage others to do the same. Caregivers and significant others can then join in savoring what precious limited time together all of us ultimately have.

Losing Touch

Dementia is a communications disorder, a condition of lost touch. The mind becomes unable to logically integrate the five senses as the afflicted individual loses touch physically, socially, emotionally, and intellectually.

We are considered cognitively intact as long as we can register and control our thoughts. Our minds and bodies are supposed to tell us when we're comfortable or in pain, hungry or happy, anxious or tired. Whenever a stimulus makes physical contact with the nerves of our eyes, ears, nose, mouth, and skin, our brain is activated. Our senses are the bridge of communication between the worlds outside and within ourselves.

As we age, we risk losing touch with the sights, sounds, tastes, and smells of the world. We can lose touch with family and friends. We can lose touch with meaning and purpose.

How we are touched is vital to our existence. A premature newborn might survive inside the warmth of a sterile incubator with artificial respiration and intravenous fluids. To thrive and develop, however, supportive human contact, physically, nutritionally, and emotionally, has to occur.

(In the 1950s, Harry Harlow, M.D., conducted social experiments using newborn monkeys. Some monkeys were provided soft cloth dolls, while others had only hard wire figurines to hold. The newborn monkeys that experienced reassurance from a comforting touch grew to function emotionally and socially. Conversely, the monkeys deprived of nurturing contact later developed physical, social, and emotional difficulties.)

The more people close in on the end of life, the more they're at increased risk of losing positive touch-related experiences. Many seniors are "handled" only for basic care or medical interventions. Without ongoing dynamic interactions, people don't thrive; they merely exist. In worst cases, elderly are sometimes subject to contact that's abusive.

Thus dementia, the disease of lost touch, perpetuates itself. Gone is sensory communication that's coordinated and sensible.

The individual with dementia progressively cannot communicate with the outside world, the outside world cannot get through to the impaired, and the body loses touch with itself.

Defining Dementia: The Technical Stuff

In this section I review some terminology and basic concepts necessary to an understanding of cognitive declines and dementia.

Dementia is an irreversible state of brain corrosion. Short-term memory loss is the most common deficit, often the first sign of cognitive decline, but memory loss alone doesn't qualify. People who suffer cognitive deficits can also lose their abilities to process or learn information, think logically, or behave reasonably or with sound judgment.

To have dementia, an individual must demonstrate deficits to the extent that his or her ability to maintain daily health and independent living is compromised. Changes in personality may also occur. Agnosia (inability to recognize objects), aphasia (inability to receive, process, or express language), and apraxia (loss of motor dexterities) are additional dementia criteria.

Dementia Criteria

+ memory loss
+ deficits in orientation, perception, intellect and learning, reasoning, abstraction, judgment
+ executive-function declines (i.e., multiple-step intellectual tasks, such as the ability to plan and execute a sequences of actions)
+ personality change
+ emotional fluctuations

- impulsive and disinhibited behaviors
- aphasia
- apraxia
- agnosia
- health, social, occupational, and personal dysfunction
- not reversible

Self-neglect is a common result of dementia and, without intervention, can lead to death. Malnourishment, dehydration, hypothermia, and health-care non-compliance are leading causes of mortality among sufferers of dementia. A confused person is at heightened risk of falling down, breaking a bone, and perhaps incurring a brain injury. Infections, falls, and consequent injuries are among the most common reasons for losing previous levels of lifestyle or function.

Dementia sufferers often deny their deteriorating condition or fail to seek assistance. Factors further complicating neuro-psychiatric declines include pride, denial, or an authentic inability to recognize or express needs. The elderly become increasingly vulnerable to exploitation.

Consequently, the early-warning signs of dementia may go unnoticed. Ultimately, it's a behavioral problem or situational crisis, and not the illness itself, that calls attention to an individual suffering from cognitive deficits.

Losing Memory

It's not uncommon that as we age, we become more forgetful. As stated earlier, forgetfulness itself is not dementia, but it is a hallmark feature. We're often concerned that losing our memory may be a sign that we're developing Alzheimer's or other cognitive decline. Remember, it's not realistic to remember everything. I qualify forgetfulness as a problem when it becomes dangerous. Absent-mindedly leaving a kitchen stove or sink unattended could cause a fire or flooding.

Forgetfulness contributes to medication confusion (and vice versa), running the gamut from not taking any at all to risking overdose. Poor memory can also affect financial accountability, resulting, for example, in the electricity or telephone being shut off due to failure to pay bills.

Usually, short-term memory loss occurs early in the course of dementia, while long-term memory remains intact through later stages. This occurrence is related to the anatomical distance of new-memory cells from their vascular roots. Sometimes, old memories become current and are confused with present reality: In this circumstance, a dementia patient is often regarded as delusional.

Forgetfulness can be both a cause and consequence of other illness. If memory loss is evident, there are likely concurrent physical and mental issues, too.

In some cases, undesirable memories may be so distressful that they turn detrimental to cognitive health and actually perpetrate dementia, which becomes preferable to an existence marred by negative thoughts and emotions.

The Four Seasons

The earliest stage of mental decline is regarded as mild cognitive impairment (MCI). The individual begins to experience forgetfulness and other subtle higher-intellect difficulties to a minor degree, but not so severe to preclude independent functioning. Self-care continues, but with less confidence and clarity. This is an opportune time for the individual to recognize and validate the changes, so proactive steps can be taken by family, community, or professional resources.

Early-stage or stage-one dementia can come to light when others more readily recognize the criteria declines. The person's ability to manage his or her own affairs comes into question. Assistance might now be needed.

There are moments of disorientation and forgetting names, information, or how to do something. Sufferers begin losing the evolved cerebral cortex skills that are superior to other animals.

This stage is also often marked by compensatory behaviors and deliberate excuse-making to cover lapses in judgment and difficulties completing the more complicated activities of modern living. In some ways it's as if the brain is neurologically reversing itself through adolescence.

Middle-stage or stage-two dementia presents with distinct declines in the parameters charted above. This period is indicated by a loss of cerebral integrity and control over moods, thoughts, and actions. Remembrances from long past begin to fill in for the short-term memory, and they become repetitious.

This stage of dementia involves a waning of the senses and sensibility, cognitive reliability, and motor dexterity. Mathematical, linguistic, and social skills are unsteady and the individual cannot sufficiently access his or her needs without assistance from others.

As stage-two progresses, dominant mid-brain function becomes more mammalian or animal-like, not unlike our domesticated pets. People with stage-two dementia still have distinct personalities and experience pleasures and threats, but they also have animal-reflex defensiveness protecting the physical and mental territories. Lost impulse control can become rather pronounced in middle dementia, resulting in wandering, falls, and lashing out at others.

Sometimes when I'm at a nursing home, a patient calls out a sound or phrase repeatedly. She isn't in pain or other distress. Rather, her mind has receded to a primitive-level nervous system, expressing itself like a bird in a tree, singing.

Stage-three-advanced or end-stage dementia is a highly digressed state of mind. Behaviors and thoughts have reverted to a basic, almost reptilian, level in terms of existence and needs. The stricken individual is alert and conscious, but often lacks social interaction or contact with his or her environment.

The essence of living is of an infant-like quality: cycles of sleeping and waking, feeding and eliminating. Oblivious to their situation, those with advanced dementia no longer possess known personalities. Total care in terms of mobility, feeding, and hygiene is provided.

Before death, there is a plant-like existence. Bodies have outlived minds.

Is Dementia Inevitable?

Questions about dementia can generate much controversial and emotional debate. Does everyone who lives long enough eventually develop dementia? Is dementia inevitable? Is it biologically predetermined? Might dementia be prevented, modified, or even reversed?

Specific answers to these questions have so far been elusive, but certain generalizations can be made. For example, our health is primarily determined by what we eat, think, and do. Genetics play a role, but so do attitude, environmental exposures, experiences, and lifestyle.

Advances in technology, health care, and pharmaceuticals have contributed to current longevity rates. Some people live beyond 100 years of age with their mental faculties intact. Others engage in unhealthy behaviors and still thrive, though they're the exceptions. Most of those who abuse their bodies pay the price. Individuals cannot afford to forfeit self-responsibility. For as long as we live, we need to actively preserve the fundamental basics of healthy living.

Using the garden as a metaphor, anyone who has tended to flowers, herbs, and vegetables knows, from experience and self-experimentation, how to maintain a proper mix of soil, fertilizer, sun, air, and water. A rich and healthy garden requires balance, diligence, and room to grow, securely.

Like all living organisms, we're programmed to live a finite number of years. Our cells eventually stop regenerating or we lose the ability to defend against illness and pestilence. The older we get, the more susceptible we become to the physical and psychological ravages of disease, including weeds of dementia that rob life from the rest of the garden.

Dementia is often preventable and modifiable. We may be powerless against time and occurrences of nature, but we're not helpless when it comes to aging with health and grace. The manner in which we apply ourselves during our peak years of adulthood determines the trajectory and velocity of our declines. Deliberately tending to good health throughout life results in a more dignified senescence.

Causes of Dementia: An Overview

Dementia doesn't "just happen." It has many roots. There is usually an identifiable underlying reason, or reasons, for a person having dementia.

Whether plant or animal, illness is caused by disequilibrium within the system. With trillions of cells in a human body, there are a lot of reasons the billions of cells in the central nervous system can fail. The human heart, lungs, bone marrow, blood cells, kidneys, liver, and essentially any organ system are all vulnerable. When the body can't support the brain, the brain can't do its job.

My medical opinion, based on years of clinical experience, is that most dementias, including Alzheimer's disease, are caused by cardiovascular (heart and blood-vessel) and respiratory (breathing) problems.

As people grow old, the heart and blood vessels become less able to maintain the necessary circulation throughout the body. Impaired or stagnated circulation distresses the brain as it undergoes deprivation of fluids, oxygen, and other essentials. Ultimately, nerve cells degenerate and die from fatigue, starvation, residue deposition, or combinations thereof.

Dementia is also caused by problems originating outside of the body. External causes include physical trauma, infection, toxins, malnourishment, medications, and substance abuse. Young people aren't immune to any of these risks.

Nervous system compromises can occur at microscopic or macroscopic levels, in select or diffuse patterns, in single or multiple locations. Furthermore, insults can occur once or be ongoing; the effects can be small and clinically insignificant or widespread and catastrophic. How a dysfunctional brain presents itself follows a primary rule of real estate: "location, location, location."

For example, frontal-lobe dementia refers to the deficits occurring at the forefront of the brain, possibly affecting cognition, social skills, and impulse control. An injury to the right lower backside of the brain causes problems with balance. An entire left-hemisphere dementia would impact language, linear thinking, and logic.

Neurovascular or cerebrovascular (brain-vessel) dementia occurs when the distribution of blood inside the brain fails. The area affected will present with motor and sensory deficits specific to that region.

Cardiovascular dementia refers to neurological declines resulting from problems with the heart or blood vessels outside the brain. Cardiopulmonary (combination heart and lung) diseases usually affect the entire brain.

Hormonal changes and deficiencies of vitamins, such as B12 and folic acid, essential amino acids, and other nutrients contribute to dementia by disrupting blood and other cell functions.

Destructive (known as neurodegenerative) changes that occur at intracellular microscopic levels are associated with Alzheimer's, Picks, and Lewy Body-type dementias. The memory loss in Alzheimer's-type declines is regarded as caused in part by inadequate production by brain cells of a neurotransmitter, acetylcholine. Parkinson's and Huntington's diseases arise from cellular deficiency in the mid-brain of the chemical neurotransmitter dopamine, which affects motor movements.

Diabetes, hypertension, and kidney failure can all cause dementia by way of disrupted metabolism and circulation. These chronic diseases often cause blood-vessel constriction, known as peripheral vascular disease. Here, your blood-vessel diameters are reduced from the equivalent size of a garden hose to that of a straw, resulting in blood-pressure and circulation irregularities. Closing off vascular circulation is the same process trees use in autumn to cut off communication with their leaves, which whither and die.

The term "hardening of the arteries" refers to the lost elasticity of aging blood vessels throughout the body and brain. Protein and fat deposits, known as plaque, line the arteries and veins, further narrowing the passageways. It becomes more difficult for the circulatory system to deliver and exchange the necessary gases, fluids, and nutrients in the brain and elsewhere. Heart attacks often occur when this kind of blockage affects the arteries that supply the heart.

Infections are capable of causing temporary or permanent brain damage. Adverse exposures to medicinal, recreational, or noxious substances in the environment, such as drugs, insecticides, chemical aerosols, smoke, and other pollutants, are some external factors. Some of the most violent behaviors I've seen in patients who qualified as having dementia due to organic brain syndromes were a result of recreational abuse from sniffing aerosols, glue fumes, or gasoline (known as "huffing"). These examples of self-inflicted dementias occurred at a very young age.

In the next section I discuss some of the more common kinds, or "species," of dementia. For more detailed descriptions, please refer to medical texts.

Types of Dementia and Related Cognitive Disorders

Mr. Williams is an 82-year-old white male admitted to an extended-care facility (nursing home) with the following diagnoses: cancer, depression, hematuria (blood in urine), primary cardiomyopathy (heart disease), hypertension, hypotension, CABG (coronary artery bypass graft surgery), hyperlipidemia (high cholesterol), constipation, and diverticulitis (bowel inflammation). Mr. William's primary diagnosis is documented as Alzheimer's disease.

This is a diagnostic profile I've seen on an actual medical chart and it's not uncommon. I frequently encounter patients who have histories of heart attacks, strokes, diabetes, head injuries, near-drowning incidents, multiple surgeries, and substance abuse, yet they incorrectly receive a diagnosis of and treatment for Alzheimer's Dementia. This occurs nationwide, daily.

Of the dozens of dementias, Alzheimer's Dementia or disease is considered the most common form. Vascular dementia is regarded the second most common type, although it's likely intimately related to Alzheimer's Dementia.

The term "Alzheimer's Dementia," however, has become as much a euphemism as an actual diagnosis. The term is used excessively, if not dismissively, not only by the public, but by professionals as well. It's not unlike brand-name recognition in the marketplace; people often say Jello when referring to gelatin or Kleenex as one brand of facial tissue. We have come to regard Alzheimer's as synonymous with dementia.

This can be quite misleading. The accuracy of a diagnosis is essential for moderating the course of an illness. As I've been emphasizing, the more we understand the roots of a disorder, the better we can manage the disease through holistic, environmental, pharmaceutical, and other supportive treatment modifications.

As I write this, earlier today I consulted on an agitated and anxious older man admitted to a long-term nursing facility. Prior to this transfer he'd been hospitalized for alcoholism and detoxified, given a diagnosis of Alzheimer's Dementia, and started on two cognitive-enhancement medications. I will calm him by discontinuing those medications and substituting a low-dose mild tranquilizer, hoping to cause the least impact on his remaining physical and cognitive health.

I'll elaborate on aging, dementia, medications, and management issues later in the book.

Alzheimer's Dementia (DAT)

Alzheimer's Dementia (also known as DAT, for Dementia of the Alzheimer's Type and SDAT, for Senile Dementia of the Alzheimer's Type) is reported to afflict an estimated five million people in the United States. The symptoms of Alzheimer's (and many other types of dementia) include memory impairment and disturbances in motor, learning, language, and recognition skills. Hallucinations, delusions, and other confusions can complicate the declines in social and personal functioning, depending on many physical and environmental factors.

The physical cause or course of Alzheimer's Dementia occurs at microscopic levels inside the brain. Deposits of protein known as neurofibrillary tangles and beta-amyloid plaques accumulate inside and around nerve cells in the brain, killing them. An analogy might be to imagine a nerve cell as a shower drain with too much hair clogging it.

Genetics and the natural aging process may play a role in the abnormal deposition of these proteins. Other considerations that may cause Alzheimer's (and other dementias) are substances we breathe, eat, drink, and absorb through our skin. Hormone changes are likely a viable contributor to dementia (they certainly matter in the lives of trees), and thus is one focus of research.

A diagnosis of Alzheimer's Dementia has historically been confirmed only after death via a brain biopsy. Protein deposits and infarcted (dead) brain tissue are recognizable microscopically in anatomical areas that correlate with the cognitive deficits.

The medical field is improving on ways to identify Alzheimer's Dementia in living brains, such as with radiographic dyes and precision photography. Even then, a dementia diagnosis needs to rely on direct assessment.

Traditionally, the diagnosis of Alzheimer's Dementia has also required that other possible dementia causes be excluded. To me, this is a key responsibility for preventing a misguided diagnosis. It's worth repeating that far too often, seniors with dementia are being diagnosed with Alzheimer's disease when, in fact, declines are really linked to underlying medical conditions, some of which may be treatable, thus ameliorating the cognitive decline. As we recall that the genesis of life is energy and circulation, we proceed with some of the most common causes of dementia and cognitive declines.

Vascular Dementia

As I related earlier, vascular dementia is regarded as the second most common type, after Alzheimer's. My experiences support that heart, lung, and circulatory problems underlie the clear majority of dementias and so I agree with the theory that these conditions most likely co-exist. These are the kinds of dementias that usually start off subtly and whose courses of decline follow the human-to-mammal-to-reptile-to-plant model of neurological devolution.

Vascular-related dementias are caused by circulatory failure. Reasons include the heart failing as a pump due to impaired strength or rhythm. Blood vessels may fail to act as conduits due to lost elasticity or tube blockage from clogging or clotting. Consequently, the brain can't get its supplies.

Blood-vessel problems can occur inside the brain or outside, or approaching it, such as the narrowing of carotid arteries in the neck. Vascular dementia is also a consequence of body-wide circulatory declines from hypertension, diabetes, and kidney disease.

If, because of systemic illnesses, a person's toes, fingertips, eyes, and other peripheral systems can't receive adequate circulation, then it stands to reason that the distant vessels in the brain will similarly suffer.

Ischemic Brain

Ischemia is a condition of tissue failure that precedes cellular death from insufficient oxygenation. Ischemia is not an official type of dementia, but it is a significant predisposition. Ischemic changes are a *very* common finding on brain scans performed to assess cognitive declines.

A common cause of ongoing ischemia is impaired breathing while asleep. I believe that sleep hypoxia, aging, and cognitive health are important enough to devote an entire chapter to it (see Chapter Four).

Over an extended period of time, poor oxygen intake is why people who have cardiovascular and lung illnesses are susceptible to developing slow, subtle, and progressive neurological declines. Severe or total airway blockages (e.g., sleep apnea) explain why many people experience strokes or heart attacks while they're sleeping.

Strokes

Inadequate oxygenation of brain tissue can occur gradually or suddenly. A cerebrovascular accident (CVA), or stroke, is a brain infarction from a sudden lack of blood supply. The consequences of a CVA depend on its location and severity. Multi-Infarct Dementia (MID) occurs when multiple brain areas are affected.

An ischemic stroke occurs from insufficient oxygen and tissue death, caused, for example, when a person suffers a heart attack and oxygen isn't adequately perfused to the brain.

Blood flow to or from the central nervous system can also be acutely disrupted when one or more blood vessels burst (hemorrhage). Strokes result from blood pressure being too high or too low, or due to medications or cardiovascular shock, among other causes. Weakening of the blood-vessel walls (aneurysm), physical trauma to the brain, and blood clots are also causes of dementia due to strokes.

Alcohol and Korsakov Dementia

Alcohol is among the oldest and most sought-after anti-anxiety substances on the planet. We drink alcohol to calm our nervous system. Its use today, as it has been throughout history, is epidemic.

A disciplined and moderate intake of alcohol is considered socially acceptable. It may even contribute to health. Inappropriate use, however, compromises behavior and bodily functions. Ultimately, the brain suffers.

The impact of excessive or inappropriate alcohol use on brain tissue can be immediately adverse. Alcohol alters judgment, which can lead to permanent and unhealthy consequences, such as physical injuries, social losses, and death to self and others. Or adversities can be hidden, taking years or decades to become apparent.

The amount or frequency of substance exposures, whether medicinal or recreational, is sometimes less of a factor than the situation when using. I might not mind if Mr. Daniels gets intoxicated once every ten years, unless, for example, he's an airline pilot and scheduled to fly the plane I'm on.

Alcohol can induce euphoria, sedation, and depression. When the initial high wears off, the body and mind are left in a weakened state. When the sedation expires, our physiology rebounds with dysfunctional excitation.

Delirium tremens, known as "DTs" or Wernicke's delirium, refers to adverse alcohol withdrawal. The mental and physical instabilities involving blood pressure, body fluids and salts, and hallucinations can be lethal if not treated correctly. Body-temperature fluctuations, violent behavior, seizure, and profound insomnia are also among the withdrawal risks. An aging body is even less tolerant of these adversities.

The long-term adverse physical effects of too much alcohol include: alcoholic cardiomyopathy, in which heart muscle made weak by alcohol cannot properly pump or conduct electrical impulses; bone-marrow suppression, causing blood-cell abnormalities; altered salt and fluid balances; pancreatic and digestive-system damage, resulting in diabetes and malnutrition; and liver cirrhosis, which disrupts blood clotting, circulation, filtering, and other metabolic functions. All these conditions impact the peripheral (outlying), autonomic (automatic, without voluntary control), and central nervous systems.

The cumulative effects of alcohol eventually impair the entire brain directly, and Korsakoff Dementia is the official term for dementia caused by chronic alcohol use. Nerves and other cells become chronically malnourished and lose their functional integrities. Being dementia, the higher-level cerebral cortex functions of intelligence, memory, reasoning, and judgment become permanently compromised.

As Korsakoff Dementia progresses, mid-brain animal-like behaviors and emotions, such as anger and anxiety, become uninhibited and impulsive. Balance and coordination are compromised in the cerebellum, as are the cranial nerves that coordinate the special senses. Patients become socially inappropriate and indifferent as the more primitive behaviors of the hindbrain become increasingly dominant.

Essentially, no component of health is left unscathed by alcohol. It's astonishingly common for patients' alcohol histories to be overlooked and inadequately appreciated as a culprit underlying a wide range of physical, social, mental, and cognitive problems.

As much as alcohol dependence is a common cause and contribution to dementia, it happens that many alcoholics never live long enough to know the experience.

Sedatives Dementia

Chemical sedatives exist in many forms besides alcohol. They're used recreationally and medicinally. They're dispensed by prescription to treat pain, anxiety, and insomnia. Potencies range from weak to lethal, from over-the-counter sleeping pills to intravenous street morphine.

Sedatives suppress metabolic activity in the brain and body and can aggravate pre-existing illnesses. Chemical sedation can contribute to delirium and permanent cognitive dysfunction.

In the short or long term, brain tissue is ultimately affected. When a threshold of inadequate cell nourishment is reached, cognitive impairments become irreversible.

Stimulants Dementia

Stimulants activate norepinephrine and dopamine neurotransmitters. Nicotine and caffeine are examples of commonly available "soft" stimulants. These, and the more potent amphetamine-related substances available by prescription and on the street, are used to accelerate metabolism for more energy and focus, happier moods, and weight loss.

Stimulants are often prescribed to stroke, heart-attack, and brain-trauma patients to promote physical rehabilitation or improved concentration. These drugs are best tolerated in modest doses and for a limited duration.

Ironically, it's not at all uncommon for a patient to receive a stimulant and a sedative at the same time, along with other medica-

tions that have a stimulating effect, such as thyroid replacements
and breathing aids.

The laws of physics, however, dictate that for every action
there must be an equal and opposite reaction. What goes up must
come down. Excessive use of stimulants can eventually deplete
neurotransmitters, causing chemical confusion or fatigue. Acute adversities of stimulants include anxiety, sleep-deprivation, impaired
sensory perception, and distorted judgment. Chronic use can lead
to hypertension, significantly adversing the kidneys, lungs, heart,
brain, and other vital organs.

As with sedatives, not only are the brain and spinal cord of the
central nervous system affected, so are the peripheral and autonomic nervous systems. Stimulants impact the voluntary and non-vol-
untary bodily functions, whether we notice or not. If not managed
correctly, cognition, mood, and behavior become erratic, leading to
eventual "burnout."

The sanctioned use of prescription stimulant drugs in America
has become alarmingly common. Their impact on families and
society is not to be ignored. These drugs play a role in helping and
hindering physical and cognitive health, whether in the patient, an
exhausted family member, or a caregiver who seeks "extra help."

Traumatic Brain Injury

Seniors with impaired vision or judgment are at particular risk
of falling. A single incident is sometimes enough to end their independent living.

Regardless of how young or old, if someone suffers blunt injury
to the brain and as a result becomes irreversibly impaired cognitively, then that person might qualify as having dementia. As we've
seen, the consequences of a trauma manifest according to the loca-

tion in the brain where it occurred.

Sometimes a head injury results in a hematoma, a type of balloon-like blood swelling that puts pressure on the brain. The sometimes-delayed after-effects range from a headache to delirium, coma, and death.

Dementia Pugilistica

Dementia pugilistica occurs from repetitious trauma to the brain. People who engage in extreme sports, such as boxing, football, and other head-jarring activities, have an increased vulnerability to cognitive declines as they age.

Parkinson's Dementia

Parkinson's disease is a neurological disorder of motor movements due to a deficiency of dopamine in the mid-brain. Dopamine is involved in our ability to move our bodies gracefully. It's also intimately related to pleasure, emotions, and perception.

Parkinson's occurs from deficiencies in dopamine production, transmission, or receptor activity. A condition known as Parkinsonism occurs from overexposure to anti-psychotic drugs or amphetamine-like substances that deplete brain dopamine; this occurrence may be as common as the biologically natural form of the disease.

Neurologic signs of Parkinson's disease include tremors that are often most pronounced in the hands. A flat facial expression can develop, motor dexterities worsen, and body rigidity sets in, compromising the ability to walk, feed, and perform other activities of daily living.

As the illness advances, the cognitive aspects of dementia begin to appear.

Lewy Body Dementia (LBD)

Lewy Body Dementia has been regarded as a variation of Alzheimer's disease, as protein deposits that accumulate in and kill brain neurons cause both. LBD often accompanies Parkinson's disease. When certain brain areas become involved, auditory or visual hallucinations may occur.

Huntington's Dementia

Huntington's disease is a neurological motor-movement disorder with a confirmed genetic-inheritance factor. Slow and squirming motor spasms can involve the entire body. As with Parkinson's, Huntington's occurs from afflictions in the mid-brain dopamine region and can progress to include cognitive failures.

Other Neurological Dementias

Examples include brain tumors that secrete abnormal neurotransmitters or encroach the brain physically, causing delirium. Diseases such as multiple sclerosis or amyotropic lateral sclerosis (ALS, or Lou Gerhig's Disease) can cause dementia as the nerve tracts lose their ability to transmit signals. Emergencies can occur when the flow of the cerebral spinal fluid becomes blocked and elevates brain pressure.

Infectious Causes of Dementia

Bacteria, viruses, and microscopic organisms known as prions are all capable of assaulting the central nervous system. Neurosyphilis, viral encephalitis, tubercular and bacterial meningitis, and Creutzfeldt-Jakob disease are less-common but still-occurring examples of dementia-causing or death-inducing invasions that start inside or outside the brain.

HIV Dementia

Dementia can be a consequence of the autoimmune deficiencies caused by the Human Immunodeficiency Virus. HIV can directly assault the central nervous system, but body-wide problems also result from the inability to fend off opportunistic bacterial, viral, and fungal infections. If unabated, cognitive and emotional problems progress as the afflicted body is weakened.

Metabolic Causes of Dementia

Kidney and liver failure are particularly hard on the brain and can cause encephalopathy ("sick brain") and altered brain function. Hyper- and hypothyroidism, diabetes, and adrenal-gland diseases are examples that, like vitamin and other nutrient deficiencies, can cause dementia if not corrected in time.

Anemia Dementia

There are many reasons why red blood cells might not function adequately: genetic, kidney, bone-marrow, and endocrine abnormalities. Poor nutrition, lack of exercise, and medication side effects are the more common reasons seniors develop anemia. Whatever the cause, impaired cells cannot transport oxygen to the brain or the rest of the body. A global dementia sets in as the brain fails to receive adequate sustenance.

Anoxic and Hypoxic Dementia

Oxygen is the most immediate element necessary for life. Only the sun, in the chronologic order of creation, precedes it. The kingdom of plants gives oxygen and all the other foods of life to us. Without oxygen we have no water.

Anoxia means no oxygen. Hypoxia means low oxygen. Hypoxemia is too little oxygen in the blood.

External causes of oxygen deprivation include near drowning,
surgery, substance-induced sedation, and high-altitude sickness.
Cigarette smoking, air pollution, and chronic lung diseases, such as
emphysema and asthma, compromise breathing. Nutrient deficiencies covertly weaken blood hemoglobin from transporting oxygen,
while carbon-monoxide poisoning does so acutely and lethally.

Fevers burn extra oxygen, compensated by hyperventilation, so
supply can meet increased demand. Sickle-cell disease and disorders
in bone marrow and other organs and systems are all subject to
oxygen dysregulation.

Sleep hypoxia may be one of the most leading but under-de-
tected contributions to cognitive declines. Years of sleeping with
low levels of oxygen sometimes manifest as dementia. Jaw malfor-
mations, deviated or narrow nasal passages, or throat obstructions
from enlarged tonsils or obesity can cause turbulent or blocked air-
flow. Seasonal and environmental allergy and sinus inflammations
are extremely common contributors to chronic oxygen compromise.

Oxygen supplementation can't reverse the irreversible aspects
of dementia, but I've seen it unquestionably help stabilize cognition,
behavior, and physical well-being.

Surgical Dementia

Surgery, like medications, can improve and save lives. Opera-
tions, however, can cause or aggravate cognitive losses. Brief or
prolonged oxygen declines can occur from anesthesia sedation or
declines in blood pressure and breathing, especially when heart
and ventilator machinery is involved. Post-surgical hypoventilation
might continue from the body being in a semi-hibernation state.

Pain and sleep medications are next dispensed, not only in the medical setting, but also to go home with, sometimes for prolonged periods.

Compromises in oxygen delivery to the brain may not be apparent or even result in cognitive loss, but hypoxic events from surgery occurring many decades earlier can predispose people to future neuropsychiatric declines. The more surgeries a person is exposed to, the more cumulative the risk for cognitive impairment.

Iatrogenic Dementia

Iatrogenic means delivery of medical care, or caused by a health-care professional. This is a fairly common contribution to cognitive declines in patients. Hospital-acquired infections, injuries, and medication errors are iatrogenic examples. Iatrogenic dementia occurs when incorrect or over-zealous treatment and medication interventions make the whole person sicker than the diagnosis.

Dementia Due to SOYA

Dementia Due to SOYA is perhaps the leading preventable cause of dementia that occurs in humans. I coined this acronym to describe the serious consequences of a sedentary lifestyle. People who do not assume the responsibility of asserting their own health are at risk for Dementia Due To SOYA.

Failure to exercise, poor eating habits, and isolation from meaningful activities lead to disuse atrophy, a medical term for body wasting from lack of use. Brain tissue withers if it isn't active. Perhaps the wisest medical advice of all is "use it or lose it," as applied physically, mentally, sexually, socially, and spiritually.

Otherwise, one risks developing SOYA: (Dementia Due To) Sitting On Your Ass.

Chapter Summary

By natural decline or catastrophe, lack of sustenance or predator assault, there are as many ways for the human body to go wrong as there are for the brain. But there are even more ways for the human body to stay healthy and active until nature really does decide otherwise. In later chapters, I address some of the approaches for navigating our cerebral destinies.

Chapter Three

ORNAMENTS AND APPENDAGES

Beautiful young people are accidents of nature,
but beautiful old people are works of art.
—Eleanor Roosevelt

Cognitive changes don't occur without affecting emotions or behaviors. The brain communicates throughout its two hemispheres, tract-to-tract, cell-by-cell, and molecule-to-molecule.

As declines in the brain start to branch out, so does that person's narrowing sensorial perception of the world. The following is a review of some of the medical, mood, and behavior problems that often co-occur as mental faculties ebb and flow.

Delirium

Delirium is an altered mental status caused by an underlying

medical imbalance. Loss of sensibilities is the brain's response to a
threatening physical problem.

Aging and natural declines can increase one's vulnerability to
physiologic imbalances. The so-called "treetops of the brain" can't
tolerate an ever-more compromised supply disruption. The body
grows less resilient to disease and gravity and seniors tend to use
more medications, adding to a risk of altered brain function.

Delirium can occur gradually or within moments of an offense
to the body. It can be obvious or subtle. For both behavioral and
medical reasons, delirium is dangerous and potentially lethal.

I was taught there are three features of delirium and that the
key diagnostic factor is that they *fluctuate*.

Fluctuations In:
  + sleep/wake states
  + motor functions
  + mental status

Alertness waxes and wanes. Motor behavior fluctuates between
calmness and agitation. Cognition and demeanor might appear rational, energized, and amicable one moment, then irrational, oblivious, and belligerent the next. Judgment and actions become inappropriate and hallucinations or delusions can occur. Both delirium
and dementia can kill due to disorganized thoughts or eventual
body breakdown.

Unlike dementia, however, delirium is reversible. When the underlying medical abnormality is corrected, mental status usually returns to its previous baseline. Untreated or prolonged delirium can
worsen cognitive problems and cause dementia. Similarly, anyone
with dementia is vulnerable to developing delirium. Prudent distinc-

tion and intervention make a significant difference in outcome.

Causes of delirium include infection, dehydration, medication toxicity or withdrawal, and inadequate oxygen. Body-salt and fluid imbalances can cause delirium. Heart attacks, strokes, cancer, trauma, and respiratory failure are often accompanied by delirium. Falling can be a cause or effect of delirium.

Delirium also occurs with drug and alcohol intoxication. Illicit, prescription, and over-the-counter pharmaceuticals all have the potential to cause an inability to think or act logically. Mixing multiple medications, alcohol, or other substances increases the risk of body failure and delirium, which are reversible, and death, which is not.

Pseudo-Dementia

False or pseudo-dementia is the term applied when an individual appears to have the signs and symptoms of dementia, but the condition is reversible. Delirium can present as pseudo-dementia, as can depression or reactions to medications. The elapsed time between recognizing and treating underlying causes of pseudo-dementia is important. The sooner a correctible medical imbalance is resolved, the less adverse the consequences. Permanent damage to the nervous system can occur if the situation isn't corrected efficiently; true dementia can then result.

Delirium, Bladders, and Bowels

The most common causes of delirium in the elderly are related to bowel and bladder dysfunctions. Insufficient fluids and medication side effects are usually at the root. Bladder infections are notorious for altering mental status in the elderly.

The annoyance and embarrassment of increased urinary frequency or incontinence sometimes cause people to drink less. Many

patients have told me they avoid drinking so they won't have to go
to the bathroom all the time. But dehydration alters bodily functions dramatically. Inadequate fluid consumption can cause blood
pressure and kidney problems or dry bowels. How many happy
constipated people do you know?

It's important to consume the appropriate types of fluids. Caffeinated beverages, for example, are diuretics. A diuretic stimulates
urination, which can result in worsening fluid and body-salt depletion. Excessive intake of milk and sugared drinks also alters the
sensitive acid-base balance of urine, increasing the vulnerability to
infections.

Many available drugs affect bowel and bladder functions. The
elderly are particularly exposed to a lot of medications that have
drying effects.

Sundowning

*It's four o'clock in the afternoon and Mrs. Eden is starting to get anxious
and irritable. Lonely, aching, and thirsty, she thinks, "Maybe those people
sneaking behind a doorway gave me some bad pills." Mrs. Eden must get out
of this strange place. Who brought her here and why?*

"Sundowning" is a term describing the decline in mental status that usually occurs in late afternoon or early evening. As the day wanes, so do the
energies and sensibilities of dementia sufferers.

Also known as Sundowner's Syndrome, confusion or memory loss becomes more pronounced. Digressions in mood, personality, and behavior
might take place. Shadows confound already impaired eyesight. If hearing is
impaired, misperceived sounds and conversations induce anxiety. Increased
emotional distress raises the risk of falling.

The distorted thought disorders of sundowning can include illusions (mis-
interpretations of existing cues or stimuli), delusions (beliefs that are not usually

Another scenario is a patient who develops an infection that causes diarrhea, which is further aggravated by the antibiotic given for treatment. Add the reduced ingestion of fluids due to nausea and you have a recipe for delirium and its accompanying risks.

Mood Disorders

Feelings are a wonderful part of life. Emotions reflect our sense of well-being or comfort. We sometimes speak of our emotions as moods and qualify them as good or bad. Moods and emotions are one way we neurologically interpret and experience the information our senses communicate to and from our brains.

Most people prefer to go through life with positive moods (feel-

---

accepted by others), or hallucinations (artificial sensory experiences conjured in the mind), any of which can result from or provoke agitation.

The aging body is more susceptible to fatigue in the afternoon, especially one that's been awake for 10 to 12 hours. Changes in blood pressure or blood sugar can also contribute to sundowning. Medications and recreational substances, such as tobacco and alcohol, that have sedative or stimulant (or both) effects on the brain can increase sundowning. Adjusting the combinations, dosages, or timing when medications are administered can mitigate the situation.

Additional ways to manage sundowning include providing a visually familiar and unobstructed floor plan and furniture arrangement, with good lighting and sound simplicity. Sometimes patients respond to a late-morning or early-afternoon rest period. Revitalized, they might enjoy a more mentally stable afternoon and evening.

More information and treatment ideas for managing sundowning are available. Ask your practitioners, look to books, magazines, and the Internet for advice, and contact community resource centers that assist senior citizens.

ings of pleasure, satisfaction, and fulfillment from love, friendship, social engagement, purpose, chocolate, etc). Ill-tempered or foul moods happen too, and they're an integral and necessary part of the human nervous system.

Clinically, moods and feelings are generally described as happy, sad, nervous, or mad. Moods might be deemed appropriate or inappropriate, volatile, erratic, or exaggerated. Moods reflect our physical and mental health and therefore can indicate if problems are occurring that necessitate a corrective intervention.

Accordingly, moods and emotions need to be regarded in their situational context. For example, lack of attentiveness (not being in the mood to pay attention) can indicate grief, an attention-deficit problem, anxiety, or depression.

As I point out later, a good health-care assessment involves appreciating the problem itself, as well as understanding the root cause. It's vital to remember that mood disturbances and their symptoms can be a reflection of psychological distress, underlying medical illness, or a sign of dementia.

Depression

Sadness is one of our natural emotions. However, when unhappiness becomes extreme or prolonged and the ability to function is impaired, it turns into a disease or disorder known as depression. Psychologically, depression is a feeling of sadness combined with a sense of helplessness.

Depression impacts hundreds of millions of people around the world. It can occur at any age, once or recurrently. It results from stresses that are purely psychological or biological, or a combination.

Depression is a common co-morbidity of cognitive declines.

Natural, healthy depression needs to be distinguished from other mood disorders, so appropriate interventions can be implemented and inappropriate treatment avoided.

For example, grief related to the deaths of loved ones significantly increases mortality among seniors. The longer we live, the more we experience losses in our lives. Responses include sadness, denial, and sometimes anger, and need to be validated and processed, while preventing despair.

In older adults especially, depression may be a symptom of covert biological imbalance, body-organ failure, or neurological problems. It's a side effect of many medications.

Social causes include financial issues, isolation, and poor support-network access. These and other stressors make vulnerability to depression greatest for those who don't practice proactive health disciplines.

Symptoms of Clinical Depression

Some people cry. Others withdraw into themselves. Some lash out. Sleep disturbances are often a prominent symptom of clinical depression, ranging from too much (hypersomnolence) to the lack of or the inability to sleep (insomnia).

Appetite disturbances can indicate depression. Inappropriate diet might include poor choices of food, overeating, or refusal. The digestive tract is highly sensitive to emotional, medical, and medication problems. Malabsorption, altered bowel movements, acid reflux, or pain can aggravate bad moods.

Depressed elders often report self-esteem declines, such as feelings of worthlessness or guilt for being a burden on others. Lack of motivation or absence of pleasures or interests (anhedonia) may arise. Changes in libido also occur with depression and could reflect more than just the hormonal, physical, and social adjustments already challenging seniors who still seek to be sexually active.

Forgetfulness, poor concentration, and anxious thoughts are also symptoms of depression. A depressed person may feel listless and dull, or conversely restless and intense. Irritability, anger, even rage can erupt or be deeply buried. Despair and hopelessness are indicators of more serious depression. Suicide is depression's ultimate expression, an act of anger and self-destruction and meant, sometimes, to punish the survivors.

Anxiety

Anxiety, fear of the unknown, is the most commonly encountered emotional challenge of the aging process. This emotion is universally regarded as inherent to sentient organisms, built on a primitive neurologic response to threatening stimuli. This feeling of nervousness or panic can warn of danger and is therefore an effective survival tool. Without some anxiety, we're overconfident and reckless. Think of anxiety as the yellow light of life.

Too much angst, however, is unhealthy and compromises the joy of living. Anxiety manifests in a person's mind, causing forgetfulness, rumination, or withdrawal. People experience difficulties in appetite, sleep, and self-control. These are virtually the same symptoms as depression, which is why these mood problems often co-exist.

Seniors fear the ongoing deterioration of physical, mental, and social health; loss of memory and concentration; of becoming isolated from people, things, and themselves; and withering away in a nursing home. Whether or not an older adult's fears of helplessness are reality based, the anxiety is valid.

Consider the emotional impact of losing one's driver's license, the ability to see or taste, or recognize the people you love. Fears of death, prolonged illness, or emptiness become more justified. You can understand why people descending into dementia might be anxious or depressed.

Familiarity and security are the opposite of anxiety. When situations or environments are foreign or perceived as unsafe, cognitively compromised people get anxious. Patients with advancing dementia consequently develop obsessions (ruminative thoughts) and compulsions (irresistible and repetitive actions). Non-pharmacologic efforts to offset these neuroses include a consistent and reassuring environment and personnel.

Accepting and being challenged by the unknown are hallmarks of psychological health. Acceptance of death, the ultimate unknown, is a crucial ingredient for successful aging with integrity.

Post-Traumatic Stress Disorder (PTSD)

PTSD is a type of anxiety disorder with particular relevance to understanding many behaviors that accompany dementia. Traumas are extraordinary experiences that threaten or cause actual harm. Acts of violence can occur naturally or by human intent, accidentally or purposefully, once or recurrently. Trauma violates and invalidates a person physically, sexually, or emotionally, and has the potential to cause significant, sometimes life-long, impact on the very roots of a person's soul.

The age of a person when experiencing trauma is a factor. A child is more vulnerable to permanent neurologic and psychiatric damage than an adult. Unresolved PTSD can lead to stunted character development, such as inflexible or maladaptive behaviors.

When PTSD occurs as a co-morbidity of cognitive confusion, it can present as a compulsive behavior, depression, or anger.

Avoidant or resistant behaviors develop, intended to prevent being reminded of past trauma. Guardedness, emotional hypersensitivity and over-reactivity, and outright paranoia can occur.

As short-term memory disappears, old memories may move to the forefront of consciousness. Anxiety, compounded by disorientation, can cause a person to believe he or she is re-experiencing the hardships. Survivors of war, poverty, or adverse immigration experiences seem particularly vulnerable. Medical problems also increase vulnerability to Post-Traumatic Stress Disorder.

When available, information about trauma history can explain why senile adults react as they do. Consider, for example, a person with dementia who resists bathtub hygiene because of a near-drowning incident that occurred decades earlier or those who exhibit hoarding behaviors because they knew extreme hunger during their youth.

Non-pharmacologic efforts to comfort PTSD anxieties include insight, empathy, and validation, and can significantly enhance the alliance between caregiver and patient.

Anxiety and Cerebrovascular Disease

Some dementias are caused by strokes that affect the ability to communicate. Stroke-induced dementias that disrupt specific areas of the brain can leave a person quite aware mentally, but unable to receive, process, or express language (aphasia). The resulting frustration or panic can be likened to being trapped behind a glass wall, where the stroke victim is desperate to make contact with the outside world, but is blocked by an invisible shield.

Personality Changes

Changes in character and behavior are often part of the dementia process. An altered personality can mean that efforts either conscious or unconscious are underway to compensate for cognitive declines. If you start losing your mental faculties, you might change your activities in an attempt to mask the losses or prevent others from detecting a problem. For example, someone who was always quite sociable might uncharacteristically avoid people or events.

Lack of impulse control, losing the ability to restrain thoughts or behaviors, is a behavioral feature of some cognitive declines. People with dementia can become emotionally inappropriate, laughing at something sad or tragic, raging over something minor, or acting melodramatically and child-like.

Relationship difficulties go hand in hand with dysfunctional personalities. Disrupting family relationships may be a sign of dementia. "Splitting," for example, is a compensating behavior that causes conflict between two or more family members, causing "good guy/bad guy" dichotomies. These behavior extremes, conscious or not, are intended to divert attention away from the cognitively compromised instigator.

Substance Abuse

Substance abuse can sometimes appear as a symptom of cognitive declines. People often self-medicate for anxiety, depression, pain and loneliness, knowingly or not.

The appropriateness of substance use is in part qualified by the consequences. Considerations include co-existing medical and medication profiles, financial affordability, and how the chemical agent affects not just the individual, but those around him or her.

Failure to Thrive

To survive, we all need life's sustenance: air, water, food, warmth, and sleep. Most of us also require intellectual, social, and spiritual activities that provide the higher qualities of life.

Dementia results in failure to thrive (FTT) when the ability to maintain one's own life with quality and independence is lost. Failure to thrive can occur insidiously, due to progressive illness, or suddenly, due to catastrophic medical and neurological events.

Dementia is sometimes only first suspected or recognized when an aging parent or patient exhibits poor judgment and an obvious decline in self-care.

Activities of daily living (ADLs) refers to our basic biological functions. To thrive, it's essential that we eat, go to the bathroom, groom, and move about.

"Instrumental" activities of daily living involve more sophisticated behaviors: using a telephone, managing finances, organizing schedules, and traveling. Instrumental ADLs require higher intellectual abilities to be intact in order for us to plan and prepare, execute tasks, and foresee consequences.

People rarely admit or volunteer that they no longer have the capacity to sustain their existence. Pride causes us to hide our weaknesses. Justifiably, we fear relinquishing our savings accounts, homes, and identities. Most of us do not want others making decisions for us. However, when it becomes apparent that mom, dad, or another close elder is not flourishing, it's time for intervention.

Decisional Capacity

Failure to thrive often co-occurs with the inability to make decisions. "Competent" is the legal term for a person who's able to understand, express, and actualize his or her own life. A person is assumed competent until proven otherwise.

Technically, cognitively impaired individuals are declared

incompetent by a court of law and not by the medical practitioner. To maintain the ethical responsibility of this serious intervention for restricting someone's freedoms, medical and legal professionals need to remember that the objective is to promote quality of life.

I'm often asked to evaluate cognitively compromised adults and seniors to determine their ability to make decisions. People who cannot adequately manage their own health, finances, and daily personal needs require someone who can. Public and private fiduciary, guardianship, and conservatorship services become involved when family members are unavailable or unwilling to assume care of the incompetent.

Common health-care concerns that raise questions of competence include consenting to or declining medical interventions, such as medications or surgery. Legal issues involving competence often involve finances, marriage and divorce, wills and trusts, selling a home, and designating a durable power of attorney.

Temporary states of incompetence occur with delirium, grief, or intoxication from drugs. These are circumstances when compromised individuals can regain capacity to thrive and make their own decisions.

"Pseudocompetence" might or might not be an actual word, but it describes the situation in which impaired people appear to possess decisional capacity, but only as a result of being under direct supervised care. Superficially intact mental faculties deteriorate quickly (within days or weeks) and result in a recurrent failure to thrive, however, upon discontinuation of the structured environment and assisted care.

Dementia, especially in early stages, doesn't automatically preclude decisional capacity. For example, sometimes a person may be capable of rational decisions regarding his health, but not his fi-

Punishing The Caregiver

As a physician, I provide care not only to an elderly or disabled patient, but also to his or her family or supporter. Caregivers come in many forms: spouses, children, friends, guardians, and a host of community and health-care providers.

As I wrote earlier in the book, sometimes patients lose touch with their own cognitive capacities and have become oblivious to their needs. Indeed, they may be like children, content to eat, sleep, and play.

The stress falls on the caregivers. Who else would pay the bills, fulfill daily and medical needs, and prevent the stricken person from wandering off in the middle of the night and freezing to death?

More challenging yet is the situation in which the caregiver becomes an object of paranoia. The person with dementia, failing to appreciate the circumstances, targets and accuses the person providing help. "My own son stole my house, my car, my money. He put me in this strange place, because he's ungrateful." Or, "Because of that no good daughter-in-law—I told him not to marry her—I'm now living in their back bedroom. They're trying to kill me."

Unfortunately, there are those who abuse or exploit the elderly. Many family and community members, however, come to the rescue of the elderly and infirm. In return for their efforts, sometimes they receive not gratitude, but assaults and accusations.

Without caring individuals, a lot of sick and old people would be in unfit conditions, alone, or not alive at all. If it weren't for the many who adjust their own lifestyles to help others, the number of people dependent on the increasingly strained social and health-care systems would be even greater.

To those who sincerely provide care to patients or their family elders, thank you. You're not alone.

nances, or vice versa. As dementia progresses, however, the stricken individual loses the ability to fulfill daily living needs and eventually develops a state of irreversible incompetence.

Ambivalence

Ambivalence, as it relates to a psychiatric component of dementia, describes an attitude of indifference as to whether one lives or dies. An ambivalent attitude may reflect an acceptance of death or a "letting go" of life when nature determines. Many are at peace with their readiness and perhaps have a desire to die, which may be justifiable for those with significantly limited life quality.

Ambivalence is not the same as an impulse toward suicide, but both may be symptoms of depression, anger, fear, or delirium.

Suicide

The risk of ending one's own life by suicide increases in later years for those incapacitated by aging. Medical illnesses, substance abuse, loss of loved ones, loss of one's own purpose, and poor access to resources compound a lack of optimism for the autumn and winter of life.

Suicide has degrees of critical intensity. Some people never consider suicide as an option. Others contemplate it, but without serious regard. Some perhaps have formulated a method, but would or could never act. Others initiate, and then thwart, their own plans. Of the people who act, sometimes a rescue is anticipated; sometimes plans go wrong. Suicide is never really "successful," medically speaking. It is regarded as "complete" or "incomplete."

In my clinical experience, I've found that depression manifesting in anger is the great indicator of the risk of suicide. As we've seen, depression can be regarded as a passive feeling of entrapment or situational helplessness. Anger, while a variant of the same perspective, is aggressive and turbulent, even when repressed.

Delirium is also a significant risk factor for suicide. Intoxication, or withdrawal from alcohol or prescription and non-prescription medications, can precipitate a suicide attempt. Physical pain or mental anguish, such as guilt or grief, can lead to suicide when duress becomes unbearable. People have killed themselves because of severe sleep deprivation that leads to delirium, irrational thinking, or profound hopelessness.

Deathics

"Don't talk about dying. You shouldn't think, let alone say, such a thing. Wishing that your life would end is immoral and reprehensible. You have to live. Even though you suffer from constant pain and have no family or meaning, we will do things to keep you alive. Because we can."

As we grow older individually and as a society, the ethical issues of quality of life and death, which I refer to as deathics, become more imminent and intimate. Try as we might, longevity with purpose and comfort can't always be achieved or maintained.

Attitudes and decisions about ambivalence, suicide, and euthanasia, especially in respect to dementia and all its co-morbidities, might be controversial, but the common goals of the quality and dignity of life remain certain. The debate over end-of-life rights is strong because we care and we want to do the proper thing.

Chapter Four

SLEEP AND DEMENTIA

We awake from every sleep except ... one ...
—Alexander Dumas

Sleep is more valuable than gold.

As written in the Book of Genesis on the fourth day, nature is cyclical. Day will follow night for as long as this sun is above this planet. Tides will ebb and flow, seasons will turn, and time will move at the speed of microseconds and eons.

Therefore, it is our destiny to wake and sleep. A necessary component of health, good sleep is satisfying, rejuvenating, and fun.

It has been my medical observation that poor sleep as a result of poor breathing is one of the most common roots underlying not only dementia, but also a lot of other illnesses.

Sleep involves giving yourself over to gravity and unconsciousness while the body recalibrates itself, physically and mentally. But loss of consciousness alone doesn't qualify as sleep. Respiration, the exchange of gases (no jokes, please), is absolutely vital for sleep, just as sleep is vital for life.

Sleep is complete when we awaken rested, with one's mental and physical energy refreshed. People thrive only when sleep is consistently and sufficiently restorative. This is true for everyone; there are no exceptions. The consensus is that people who sleep well and for appropriate hours tend to live longer.

Much about sleep remains a mystery. We know that it's a necessary biological function basic to all animals. We also know that our brain goes through a series of wave processes, dream stages, and stuff like that.

Acute sleep deprivation can be invigorating in the very short-term, but after a while it causes undue strain on the brain and the body. Eventually, we become so mentally or physically deranged, we collapse.

Most people require between six and eight hours of sleep in a 24-hour period. Sleep requirements and patterns might change in aging adults, but some amount of sleep is always required every day.

Everyone sleeps, some. Some sleep well; others have difficulty. No one never sleeps. When patients tell me, "I *never* sleep," I validate that they lack healthy slumber. But without ever sleeping, they'd be psychotic in three days and dead in about a week.

Older adults often report a reduced quantity and quality of sleep. As we age, impaired sleep may also be attributed to poor general health or frequent naps ("*I never sleep during the daytime … I just close my eyes and rest for a few hours*"). Impaired vision and hearing, pain, and disorientation further compound seniors' vulnerabilities to problems with "normal" sleep.

Failure to exercise, effects of medication, and unhealthy dietary habits underlie most sleep problems. Sleep-deprivation-by-proxy happens to people who share their beds with partners with sleep disorders. Equally important are our spiritual, social, psychological, and intellectual stimulations. Universally, those who are actively engaged in life sleep the best.

Sleep can become excessive in the presence of boredom and the absence of mental challenge and social stimulation. In advanced dementia, people regress to the extent that they mainly eat, eliminate waste, sleep, and breathe.

Sleep and Oxygen

Oxygen is kind of important. Our brains require 20% of our oxygen intake. We can live, at most, five minutes without oxygen. Like a tree's topmost leaves that depend on roots to provide nourishment, our nerve cells way up in the nether regions of the brain depend on the rest of the body to circulate oxygen and water, awake or asleep.

Sleep difficulties remain a top health concern in many cultures. Insomnia is one of the most common health complaints heard at a doctor's office, yet chronic sleep-oxygen deficiency is too-often overlooked as a cause of sleep and cognitive disorders.

Hypoxia is the condition of insufficient amounts of oxygen in the body (hypoxia) or blood (hypoxemia). Intermittent, partial, or full obstruction of breathing causes sleep hypoxia due to sleep apnea (without breath) or hypopnea (reduced breathing rate).

Impaired sleep oxygenation may occur occasionally or can continue for years, if not over a lifetime. This at times not-so-silent event erodes the mind and body, causing cognitive declines and outright dementia.

The brain wants you to know, from the bottom of its heart, it appreciates all the oxygen it can get.

Seasons, Sneezin's, and Other Reasons

Years of abnormal breathing can lead to a host of physical, emotional, and cognitive deficits. Conditions of oxygen inadequacy can present as attention deficit, hypertension, and gastro-esophageal reflux. Heart attacks and strokes are often associated with middle-of-the-night oxygen declines.

Social, family, and professional functioning can be severely compromised when respiratory problems are aggravated by insomnia. Your emotional and physical stress levels feel exaggerated and out of proportion with your life. Moods and behaviors can be dysfunctional or erratic. These symptoms can lead to the desperate abuse of substances for inducing sleep.

Poor concentration and focus, memory loss, and irritability, when caused by chronic oxygen deprivation, often look a lot like dementia or delirium.

Bizarre dreams occur, in part, due to agitation of the central nervous system caused by low levels of oxygen. Some people awaken anxious and breathing rapidly, thus replenishing their oxygen intake.

Another symptom of sleep hypoxia is the sensation of rarely or never feeling quite rested. A sufferer often takes frequent or spontaneous daytime naps to compensate. Nocturia (the frequent need to urinate during sleep hours), restless leg syndrome, and headaches might be associated with low oxygen levels and consequent lack of restituted energy expected from sleep.

Uncommonly, sleep disorders arise from neurological trauma or disease, such as narcolepsy. Much more common are anatomical problems. People with swollen nasal sinuses, a deviated septum, enlarged tonsils, or nose or jaw fractures are particularly susceptible. Being overweight can also physically impede breathing. Respiratory problems from cigarettes, seasonal and pet allergies, and other environmental toxins often interfere with proper breathing. Sleep posture affects airway passages, especially for those who twist their airways to breathe while asleep on their stomach.

Other causes of sleep disturbances include pain, not enough hours allotted, or a prohibitive environment, such as a companion who snores like a rhinoceros. Stress, depression, and anxiety significantly impact both sleep quality and quantity.

Elderly patients have additional vulnerabilities to sleep hypoxia. Aging blood vessels are apt to become less elastic. The lungs and heart have less vitality. Perfusion is compromised and the brain doesn't get what it needs.

Dementia can upset the sleep-and-wake cycle due to time disorientation. I once assisted with managing a man who was admitted to a nursing home because of significant dementia. He never slept well at night and was disruptive to the others. One root of his confusion? He'd worked the nightshift, most of his life.

An Early Winter: Consequences of Poor Sleep

People who experience chronically poor sleep live a life that falls short of what it could be. It's like a plant that never gets enough sunlight or water. There is existence, even growth, but it can't realize full bloom and color.

Trauma

Sleep disorders substantially increase the risk of accidental harm to oneself and others. An estimated three million annual automobile crashes are attributed to sleep hypoxia or the seda-

tives used in its treatment. Untold mishaps occur when we're sleep
deprived.

Heartaches, Headaches, and Stroke

Heart attacks and cerebrovascular accidents (CVA, a.k.a
stroke) often occur in the middle of the night when a person's respirations and oxygen consumption get too low. High blood pressure
and abnormal heart rhythms can occur to compensate.

Headaches often result from poor sleep. It makes sense that
sleep is a powerful headache remedy.

Delirium

Total sleep deprivation results in delirium. The body, exhausted, begins to biologically shut down. After somewhere between
thirty-six and seventy-two hours of not sleeping, we start dream-
ing while awake. We hallucinate and become psychotic, leading to
grave endangerment from impaired judgment and behaviors. The
probability of death from lack of sleep rises to near inevitability
after about seven days.

Partial but chronic oxygen deficiency can cause aggression and
other inappropriate behaviors. The nervous system is off-center just
enough to generate paranoia in some people.

*Adam was diagnosed in his early twenties as having paranoid
schizophrenia, after an alcohol-induced psychotic episode involving his
Post-Traumatic Stress Disorder. Twenty years later he was hospitalized
because of paranoia and agitation occurring in the middle of the night.
When I evaluated him, I learned that he'd been a boxer in youth and
incurred several nose traumas. He acknowledged chronic congestion,
sinus allergies, and restless sleep with distressful dreams and physical*

thrashing, in spite of his many psychiatric medications.

Yes, he answered, he'd always been told he snored like a moose!

I prescribed his hospital bed be elevated to a semi-upright angle, with supplemental oxygen by nose tubing at bedtime. His psychiatric medications were reduced and dispensed only at bedtime, using to advantage their side effects of mild sedation and dryness, the latter which alleviated the inflammation of his nasal and respiratory passages.

I remember the morning after this treatment. Adam said it was the first time in years, if ever, he'd awakened refreshed. Adam's mental health significantly improved. In effect, he was provided with sufficient breathing while asleep, an experience he'd been lacking for decades.

Mood Disorders

Emotional stability is predicated on cognitive stability, and both are dependent on adequate sleep. I've just illustrated how sleep hypoxia can exacerbate a thought disorder. Depression, anxiety, and manic-depressive (bipolar) mood swings can also be triggered by disrupted sleep and oxygen.

Stress takes a physical and psychological toll on our thoughts and ability to relax. Symptoms similar to mood disorders and sleep hypoxia include disturbing dreams, gasped awakenings, rapid heart-beat, and frequent trips to the bathroom to urinate.

Seasonal Affective Disorder (SAD) is triggered in some patients by seasonal allergies that disrupt sleep. Consistent with nasal irritation and reduced oxygen flow, many people become depressed or anxious on windy or high-pollen-count days.

This is a good place to emphasize that sleep and other medical disorders *do not* explain all mental-health disorders. It's sometimes worthwhile to confirm that sleep hypoxia doesn't exist and isn't an underlying aggravator. Patients with Post-Traumatic Stress Disorder, for example, could be fearful of sleep due to purely psychological reasons, such as nightmares or paranoia.

Substance Abuse

Desperation for sleep drives many people to drink and take pain relievers and sleeping pills. Excessive reliance on substances, however, usually becomes a vicious cycle. Tolerance to usual doses develops, triggering the need for increased amounts.

Sedatives promote unconsciousness, but they also sedate nerves, muscles, metabolism, and vital body functions. Used properly and sparingly, a sedative-hypnotic can restore and prevent illness; otherwise, it worsens the original sleep problem.

Evening cocktails can innocently but inadvertently disrupt sleep. Any sedative exposure in the late afternoon can cause sleepiness hours before one intends to retire for the night. The relaxation wears off, but the natural sleep cycle has been interrupted. The gap between waking and sleeping has been compromised, thus causing a re-awakening or "second wind."

People who do fall asleep at night from the effect of alcohol often report jolting awake around two o'clock in the morning. This seems a universal response among sedative, hypnotic, and analgesic agents taken at bedtime.

Therefore, a good first step is to recognize whether alcohol or another chemical relaxant (or, in some cases, its absence) is contributing to a sleeping problem or is being used as a precipitous effort to get some sleep. If so, its use may need to be modified.

Attention Deficit

I contend that children and adults who present with attention deficit and other disorders of concentration need screening to rule out sleep hypoxia and environmental factors. People with enlarged tonsils, nasal congestion, or other anatomical breathing compromises can be forgetful and restless and lack impulse control.

Foods and stimulating beverages before bedtime are common behavioral culprits, as can be television or computer activities that rev up instead of calm down.

A person's living situation is another consideration in determining if viable sleep is occurring. Sleep is best in an environment secure from physical or psychological harm and thus absent of the need to be hyper-alert.

Attentiveness problems worsen if the underlying reasons aren't correctly identified and alleviated. Often, inappropriate, even aggressive, treatment ensues, such as medications that may provide symptom relief, but covertly worsen the body in the long term.

Restless Leg Syndrome

Restless leg syndrome is another symptom of poor oxygen delivery while asleep, and can get better with improved sleep hygiene. A burning sensation develops in the muscles due to a chemical buildup of lactic acid when oxygen levels are low. The body reacts with involuntarily leg movements, which increase respirations and vascular circulation.

Some medicines help by promoting circulation, replenishing nutrients, or suppressing pain. On the other hand (or leg), depending on the cause and accuracy of the diagnosis, medications might relieve the restlessness, but bring about adversity to the brain or other organ system.

GERD

The gastro-esophageal sphincter is a valve that requires adequate oxygenation to effectively close off stomach-content regurgitation. Gastro-Esophageal Reflux Disease (GERD) occurs when acid from the stomach irritates the throat.

Dietary issues are considered and, frequently, stomach-acid-relief medications are initiated. It helps to assess whether sleep hypoxia is also partly responsible.

An elevated sleep position treats GERD by promoting gravity's pull against acid reflux. A semi-upright posture can also improve oxygen intake.

Inquiring Further

When I assess patients' sleep relative to their cognition, I ask about their subjective symptoms. Do they usually awaken refreshed or not? Do they in general feel fit or, instead, physically or mentally out of proportion to an otherwise satisfactory life?

I inquire about snoring or turbulent breathing patterns, restlessness, or nighttime urination. I inquire about physical anomalies, such as facial traumas, surgeries, deviated septum, allergies and pet exposures, smoking, and medications.

I ask patients to summarize their use of alcohol and other substances.

Behaviors such as a nocturnal lifestyle, eating late, or sedentary nights in front of a television or computer may be pertinent. Sometimes I inquire about past traumas that occurred at night, which might be associated with psychological anxiety surrounding sleep or darkness. Dream disturbances could reflect the coexistence of both psychological and physical problems.

While asking questions, I observe the patients' physical health and appearance. I register their mental and cognitive functions, such as mood, behavior, thought processes, the ability to "think straight," and their neurological coordination.

When available and appropriate, I can incorporate medical information from diagnostic analyses that include blood samples, pulmonary-function tests, cardiograms, and magnetic resonance imaging (MRI). Oxygen levels in the blood are measurable and sleep clinics can observe, qualify, and quantify sleep disorders.

Laboratory findings serve to guide diagnosis and treatment, but the human element always needs to be prioritized. Based on my experiences, I believe the clinically sophisticated sleep and oxygen studies too often fail to validate the presence of a sleep-related oxygen deficiency. Computer-generated test conclusions might indicate the patient didn't qualify as "apneic" enough, or the blood oxygen carriers (hemoglobin) didn't "desaturate" enough, but I'm not always convinced that the entire brain is getting enough oxygen.

The final analysis is reached when the history, examination, and laboratory studies are reviewed. Then it's time to make a diagnostic conclusion and decide a plan of treatment.

If all else fails, I *look* at the patient. Does he or she appear more tired than me?

Treating Sleep Disorders

The symptoms I've described in this chapter may be applicable to you or someone you know. Recognizing this possibility can indicate further evaluation. When people ask me what they should do to determine if they have a sleeping problem, I suggest that they might first educate themselves by reading books or websites for objective information that isn't selling anything.

The next step in treatment for a sleep-apnea or hypopnea-related disorder is professional verification. Doctors can recommend various interventions, according to the root and severity of the sleep disturbance.

Non-Pharmacologic Interventions

Simple behavioral adjustments may not always help, but they rarely cause harm. Overall lifestyle modifications, including proper diet and exercise, improve most sleep problems; therefore, these are the most successful and non-invasive treatments. Reducing excessive body weight and quitting smoking also contribute to more efficient respiration, relieving pressure on the chest and strain on the heart. Also, some of you need to stop letting your cat sleep on your head.

Reassurance is another natural intervention. A law has never been written that says we must sleep only at night and all in one session. Some people thrive on split hours, such as sleeping four hours, awake eight hours, asleep four hours. Physical illness that splinters sleep may still prove sufficient, as long as the total amount in twenty-four hours is reasonable.

However, disciplined sleep schedules are often helpful. When feasible, consistent sleeping and waking hours reinforce the body's metabolic rhythms. Daytime naps may be healthful, as has been noted in cultures in which mid-day sleepers experience a lower incidence of heart disease.

It's helpful to complete naps before 2 p.m. to avoid compromised sleep during the night ahead. Try not to fall asleep in the evening while watching television; do something else.

The quality of a mattress or the bed's location in a room may need adjustment. A fan or noise machine may miraculously harmonize snoring with the sound of the ocean. Sexual activity is often a prelude to better sleep. It's often encouraging to know that it's natural to sleep more in autumn and winter, consistent with longer nighttime hours of darkness.

An improved sleeping posture is enough to provide benefit. Many people sleep best when *not* on their backs, a position notorious for snoring. Perhaps sitting upright while sleeping may be a lost instinct we once shared with large primates. Raising the head of the bed may relieve weight from the chest and improve throat alignment. A vertical elevation significantly reduces sinus pooling and congestion for some, especially those who report copious nose blowing when they wake in the morning.

Hospitalized or medically bed-bound patients are vulnerable to intermittent napping and sometimes extremely frustrating nighttime sleep. Sometimes people who sleep in five-minute spells throughout the day do so from boredom or medication. Physical, intellectual, and social activities can help alleviate this problem.

A more open nasal airway can be achieved by placing breath-assisting bandages designed for placement across the nose. Dental devices and neck-support pillows might improve breathing.

I often favor oxygen treatment because I see it improve sleep and cognitive quality. Pure oxygen, which is technically a prescription drug, can be delivered through nasal-canal tubing worn under the nose or a lightweight mouth-breathing mask. Benefit is subtle and unlikely to reverse years of ischemia, but it's rewarding to see a patient's overall demeanor get brighter in response to oxygen supplementation.

Continuous Positive Airway Pressure (CPAP) involves wearing a mask smugly on the face to allow a tight seal for air delivery. This, and the BiPAP variation, can be literally life restoring for some, while for others it's the most intolerably annoying device ever invented. Perhaps hyperbaric oxygen treatment will someday play a greater role in treating cognitive declines.

Rarely, excessive oxygen supplementation could prove lethal in people with very severe respiratory disease who retain carbon dioxide.

Surgical and laser interventions include deviated-septum repair, tonsillectomy, and correction of a misaligned jaw. A more intensive procedure involves surgically widening the vault of the throat, known as uvulopharyngoplasty.

I might prescribe sleeping upright as a first step, then the uvulopharyngoplasty.

Medications and Sleep

Sedatives

The following is a review of prescription medications often involved with sleep issues affecting seniors and not-so seniors. Many of these medications are mentioned again later in the book in the medicating dementia section (see Chapter Nine), a testament to their prevalence and variability of use.

Artificial sedation has been a human behavior for a long time; it's the means by which many people relax at the end of a day. Sedative substances are abundant and include agents whose potencies and efficacies vary, whether found in nature or on the pharmacy shelf. Benefits and cautions apply to all.

Hypnotics are agents meant to specifically induce sleep. Sedatives secondarily induce sleep by their calming actions.

Sedatives are available recreationally, by prescription, and over the counter as antihistamines, cough syrups, and anything else that qualifies as a sleep aid.

Prescription sedative-hypnotics include benzodiazepines and their variations, serotonin and melatonin enhancers, opiates, muscle relaxants, barbiturates, and other tranquilizers.

The same apothecary for sleep is also known in the forms of anti-depressants, antihistamines, anti-anxiety (anxiolytics, minor tranquilizers), muscle relaxants and analgesics (pain relievers), mood stabilizers (thymoleptics), and anti-psychotics (major tranquilizers, neuroleptics).

The newest sleeping agents have propelled the sedative divisions of pharmaceutical companies into multibillion-dollar enterprises.

In most situations, sedative agents work best when taken occasionally and briefly. Preferably, sleeping pills are used judiciously to enhance rest until the true reason for the insomnia has been corrected. Sedatives can be habit-forming, so long-term and continuous usage is reserved for unusual circumstances, such as when discontinuation would cause serious medical or psychological withdrawal.

Sedatives are aimed at suppressing a select central nervous system action. However, they're not as specific to sleep as drug-company marketing and advertisements would have us believe. As I've mentioned, the autonomic and peripheral nervous systems can also be sedated, slowing the heart, lungs, and digestive tract. There's also suppression of biochemical activity at the cellular level.

Sedatives can accumulate in the body, causing subtle physical and psychological dependence. They also alter the activities of other medications. Cognitive disruptions can occur or become worse. Confusion or forgetfulness becomes prominent, as physical and mental energies are subdued.

Daytime use of stimulants, pain-relief medications, and muscle relaxants frequently affects sleep schedules and quality. This increases the chance that a patient will receive a sleeping pill. Once again, seniors with compromised health and multiple medications are most vulnerable to the synergistic consequences.

Prescribed sleeping agents are sometimes used concurrently with non-prescribed stimulants, such as evening coffee or soda. Some people aren't kept awake by caffeine. Most, however, do best to avoid mixing them. The experience is usually a restless drowsiness, a feeling also associated with antihistamine-type medicines.

People might take their sedative medications too early before bedtime. As with alcohol, sleep is induced prematurely, the sedation wears off, and the night hours are restless. When sedatives wear off, people often experience a discomforting rebound. Anxiety and insomnia can become worse than before.

That's why another factor in prescribing medication is the time of day when the patient takes it.

Also, like alcohol, most sedative-hypnotics are effective for several hours, causing a rebound awakening between one and three o'clock in the morning. Some people develop the habit of taking an additional sedative in the wee hours. If a person thrives or is at least functional with this behavior, there may not be a problem.

(If it ain't broke, don't fix it. Some of my patients have taken their medications for so many years that to try to reduce or discontinue them would cause more disruption than benefit.)

Newer sleeping agents combine immediate and delayed-release activity. This can result in the medication lingering, impairing alertness and bodily functions during the day.

Combining sedatives is very dangerous. A sleeping pill, along with narcotics for pain and a liquid antihistamine with alcohol for sinus congestion, can be lethal. A clinical approach to appreciating cumulative effects of combinations, especially with seniors, is to remember that one plus one equals three.

Prescription Sleepers

Sleeping pills are safe and effective when used properly, but need to be respected for their potential. Voluntary users of sleeping pills must shoulder the responsibility for remaining informed about these and *all* their medications, while the cognitively impaired need to be protected. Ask your practitioner for the "big picture" on these medications. Beware of free samples and prescriptions that include an excessive number of refills in the absence of monitoring. Evaluate the long-term side effects of any sedative and attempt to resolve the underlying cause of the insomnia.

As stated, first-line interventions for preserving sleep are preferably natural, but the reality in today's world is that a preponderance of seniors are taking a preponderance of prescription agents for sleep. The following is neither an extensive or inclusive list, but demonstrates there is no medication shortage at the drugstore.

Benzodiazepines (BZD)

I consider this class of medication as "alcohol in pill form"; their actions are virtually the same. Both are calming and relieve anxiety. BZDs are used to detoxify people off of alcohol and to curb aggressive behaviors in patients with advancing dementia.

Benzodiazepines are among the most basic target-specific prescription drugs. These sedative-hypnotics have been used for more than fifty years to treat nervousness and sleep and they really are relatively safe and effective.

But the truth is BZDs are chemicals and they alter our metabolism. Used prudently, side effects of over-sedation, confusion, forgetfulness, pseudodementia, falling down, hypotension, respiratory arrest, coma, and death can be avoided. Paradoxical reactions to benzodiazepines include ambivalent and uninhibited behaviors, such as violence or panic over the feeling of a loss of self-control.

Benzodiazepines vary in terms of potency, speed of onset, and duration of effect, and are subject to one's metabolism and other medications. Several of the common brands are as follows.

Triazolam (Halcion) and temazepam (Restoril) are shorter-acting agents that promote faster sleep onset. Alprazolam (Xanax) is also quick in onset, but it too is short-lived. Lorazepam (Ativan) has a medium range of potency and duration. Diazepam (Valium) and clonazepam (Klonipin) are longer acting.

Extended-release versions of some benzodiazepines are also available.

GABA (Gamma-Amino-Butyric-Acid)/BZD

Drug companies are spending millions of dollars to advertise and market the more recent sleeping agents zolpidem (Ambien), eszoplicone (Lunesta), and zaleplon (Sonata). The claim is that these sedatives selectively activate the gaba-amino-butyric acid (GABA) receptors, as opposed to affecting benzodiazepine receptors. Neurologically, the GABA and benzodiazepine receptor sites are quite similar.

The risk-and-benefit profiles of the new drugs are the same as the benzodiazepines, but they cost more. Patients validly respond to or prefer one type to another for reasons that include a placebo effect, as well as actual biochemical reactions.

Many GABA medications used for seizure control are also used for psychiatric and dementia-related behavior management. Divalproex (Depakote), carbamazepine (Tegretol), gabapentin (Neuron-

tin), and others have sedative activity, which are potentially beneficial when prescribed correctly.

Melatonin

Ramelteon (Rozerim) is being marketed as enhancing melatonin activity, a central-nervous-system hormone that is closely associated with sleep. It may be no more unique than non-prescription
less-expensive melatonin supplements from the organic-food store.
Rozerim is marketed to be taken on a consistent basis, which seems
counterintuitive to the preferred occasional use of sleep aids.

Anti-Psychotics (Also Known As Neuroleptics and Major Tranquilizers)

Haldol, Thorazine, Mellaril, Navane, and Stelazine revolution-
ized modern psychiatry's ability to manage schizophrenia illnesses
and psychotic episodes. More recent entries in the market include
the very expensive and doubtfully superior aripiprazole (Abilify),
quetiapine (Seroquel), ziprasidone (Geodon), olanzepine (Zyprexa)
and risperidone (Risperdal).

These drugs work by sedating mental and physical aggression.
Insomnia alone is usually not an adequate justification for prescribing these potent drugs, but many of the anti-psychotics have
sedation side effects, especially advantageous when sleep is a desired
piece of the treatment puzzle.

Antidepressants

When used appropriately, antidepressants that induce drowsiness might be a less-potent chemical alternative than other sedatives and tranquilizers for improving sleep and other mood-related
features.

All antidepressants, however, have the potential for not only neurological and psychiatric side effects, but also gastrointestinal reactions. Many of the same neurotransmitters exist in the brain, digestive tract, and elsewhere. In addition to many seniors already being sensitive to appetite changes or irregular bowels, other side effects of antidepressants, new and old, can include headache, tremor, altered mental status, and depression.

Trazodone (Deseryl) is an older antidepressant that can be dosed as a sleep aid. Very rarely, priapism (a painful penile erection due to blood entrapment that can become a medical emergency) has been attributed to trazadone (and other psychiatric medicines).

Trazadone is related to but slightly different than the tricyclic antidepressants (TCAs) that have been around about as long as the benzodiazepines and older antipsychotics. The tricyclic antidepressants useful for sleep include amitriptyline (Elavil), doxepin (Sinequan), and imipramine (Tofranil). Sometimes effective for treatment of nerve pain, they can be very drying and induce sedation, but they can also paradoxically cause restlessness. Other related TCAs arguably tend to have more of an activating than calming effect.

The next development in antidepressants focused on promoting serotonin, a known neurotransmitter that exists in nature and makes animals sleepy. Fluoxetine (Prozac) was among the first selective serotonin reuptake inhibitor (SSRI) antidepressants, but it seems to boost energy and is usually taken in the morning. SSRIs like sertraline (Zoloft), citalopram (Celexa and its variant Lexapro), and paroxetine (Paxil) appear to relax people who may take them during the day to feel calmer or before bedtime if it helps them sleep better. People respond differently and have preferences.

Other recently introduced antidepressants, such as venlafaxine

(Effexor and its variant Pristiq), duloxetine (Cymbalta), and mirtazapine (Remeron), are known for their combination of stimulant and suppressant activity at multiple brain receptor sites. My opinion is that these are less often a first choice for dual treatment of mood and sleep in elderly. Some patients do respond to these mixtures, but most seniors can tolerate only so many uppers and downers coursing through their arteries and nerve endings at the same time.

Analgesics

Sleep is an analgesic, a pain reliever. All of the above-listed medications could be regarded as pain relievers.

Chemical analgesics range from a mild anti-inflammatory such as aspirin, originally derived from the bark of a tree, to a strong narcotic such as morphine, originally derived from the seed of a plant.

Opiates, barbiturates, morphine, codeine, and other narcotic derivatives are potent. We know some of these agents as Fioricet, Vicodin, Tylenol with codeine, Ultram, and cough syrups with hydrocodone. They act by blunting pain receptors and promoting the release of the nervous system's own analgesics. They give relief to sufferers, thereby restoring the opportunity to participate in various activities. Narcotics initially cause euphoria, but then the user gets sleepy.

Coordinating the use of these agents with periods of sleep can help preserve the sleep-wake cycle. Narcotics can really knock a person out, but their body-wide side effects are stronger too. Delirium with paranoia and hallucinations are among the more serious psychotic reactions, especially challenging as these powerful tranquilizers are often involved with hospice and end-of-life management.

Diphenhydramine

I conclude this chapter by discussing one of the most prominent pharmaceutical agents available, diphenhydramine. A very versatile drug, it's available over the counter, as well as being present in a lot of prescription medications. This is the generic name of the active ingredient in Benadryl, the "PM" in non-aspirin pain relievers, and a host of others, some of which are likely in your medicine cabinet now.

Diphenhydramine-related drugs can save lives when used to reverse severe medication allergies. The drug works in part by causing blood-vessel contraction (vaso-constriction) throughout the body, which helps dry a runny nose, reduce a seasonal-allergy inflammation attack of sneezing, or contain the swelling after a bee sting.

Anti-cholinergic drugs like diphenhydramine are extremely commonly used for sleep. They are sedating initially, but people often experience a "tired-but-wired" reaction. They can also induce a physiologic dependence.

Judicious occasional use can be beneficial, but this universally available medicinal agent can cause constipation, urinary retention, cardiovascular changes, and prominent mental imbalances, such as reduced alertness and cognition, irritability, and delirium.

Chapter Summary

We sleep about one-third of our lives, so it makes sense to breathe adequately during this activity. Compromised breathing while asleep is a prominent but often unrecognized culprit that underlies many medical problems, including dementia.

Treatments range from simple and natural interventions to

more invasive procedures. Sedatives promote sedation but can often suppress biological functions, so be sure the sleep-promoting initiatives don't aggravate a situation.

Sleep is as essential as sunshine, oxygen, water, and food and should be as natural as day and night. At least once per twenty-four hours, we need complete sleep with air if we want full wakefulness.

The happiest people on the planet get enough sleep.

PART TWO

GETTING OLDER AND DEALING WITH IT

Chapter Five

GEROLESCENCE

The trees that are slow to grow bear the best fruit.
—Moliere

Life's too fun to be short.
—Me

Adolescence is the phase of life between childhood and adulthood. "Gerolescence" is a term I coined to describe the phase of life between middle and late adulthood. I have discovered that applying the theme of gerolescence to my patients and myself enhances physical and mental health.

If adolescence is like the springtime that prepares us for the summer of our lives, then gerolescence is the autumn that will deliver us into winter. It's the geriatric adolescence, an epic period of transformation and a true opportunity to "grow up" again.

We sprout through youth, expanding and branching out through adulthood until we reach full maturity. Like the changing leaves on a tree at summer's end, gerolescence is a time to prepare for one's brilliant display of fall colors.

Adolescent experiences are a vital and ongoing rehearsal for shaping who we eventually become as adults. Decades later, by recalling our origins and youthful experiences, we can get the most out of our senior seasons.

Adolescence

The start of adolescence is capricious. A genetically set hormone awakens from biological dormancy while we're asleep, or at 2:15 in the afternoon, just because. Some cultures celebrate and welcome adolescence with a social or religious ceremony. Others arbitrarily mark it by age, such as twelve years old.

Adolescence is a time of significant growth. We enter as children and only six to eight years later graduate as adults. Compared to some of the other developmental phases, that's a relatively short time span. Teenagers are challenged to quickly merge with and adapt to an increasingly complex world without killing themselves. Survival requires the acquisition and mastery of neurocognitive and behavioral skills built on those we had as children.

Change, The Only Constant

Every moment that passes in life is a loss and a gain, a death and a birth. By the time we reach adolescence we've experienced a lot of both. We ceased crawling when we started walking. We began middle school and said farewell to the elementary years. We've said goodbye to pets, people, and innocence and hello to the bittersweets of reality. Adolescence mourns the loss of childhood security and its expectations and celebrates the becoming of an autonomous adult.

Puberty is a time when secondary sexual characteristics develop, announcing itself through physical changes in voice and appearance. Non-physical changes in mood, thought, and behavior are consistent with the adolescent urge to respond to accelerating neurological and body-wide development, raging hormones, and personal and social identity challenges.

Identity

Adolescence is a period of identity formation and validation: Who am I, where do I come from, what is my place in the world, and where is my life going?

The teenage years are a time of experimentation. How we dress, our beliefs and values, whom we associate with, our music are all chosen to describe, reflect, and express ourselves. Nature and people around us are ongoing factors. Unfortunately, some of us suffer traumatic invalidations or abuse.

We compose our adolescent personalities by simultaneously rebelling against and imitating the identities, philosophies, and actions of peers and role models. Sometimes, as teenagers, we act responsibly. Other times we're irresponsible, just like our adult mentors. Experiences and the consequences of our actions hinder or reinforce growth as we refine ourselves in context to the rest of the forest.

Hobbies, Talents, and Interests

When we're young, most of us have some kind of artistic, musical, athletic, physical, or intellectual interests and talents. As teenagers, we explore our imagination, dreams, and aspirations. We learn that education comes from both academics and real-life experiences. We establish relationships and discover pastimes and causes that are meaningful to us.

Adaptive abilities grow by necessity. Others give us validation

or happiness. Some are a calling or a natural-born gift. It takes skill
for an adolescent to survive into adulthood and talent to bloom.

Conflict and Conformity

As we mature, we gain power and confidence to make decisions. We discover that choices have consequences, good and bad.
We realize what we can and cannot control. We develop a sense
of whom to trust and when. We learn about independence and
interdependence.

The conflicts of adolescence often involve rebellion against con-
formity. A budding adult naturally pursues peers and activities that
reinforce and validate his or her perspective on reality. For many
adolescents, rejection of family or social norms is a necessary part of
the search for identity and personal empowerment.

Teenagers often oppose practical advice, spurned in favor of the
pursuit of individual ideals and the drive to know for themselves.
To the best of their abilities, adults need to provide children and
adolescents a governed atmosphere, while new judgment aptitudes
and nerve buds are still developing.

The Death of Adolescence

At the conclusion of our adolescent years, we've turned into
young adults, ready to reach our potential and be a part of the
world. Hopefully, we've gained sufficient understanding about the
realities of life.

With the death of adolescence also comes an end to wishful
thinking. Mature adolescents and adults learn that we can do *anything* we want, but we cannot do *everything*. We know we can try to
do whatever we choose, but we have to commit to the labor.

Anything worthwhile requires effort. Living isn't free; shelter, food, transportation, and everything else in life have costs. We grieve the death of youthful innocence when we accept the constancy of change. We must now earn our pleasures to know happiness.

The Birth of Adulthood

At the end of youth, who we've become is physically and mentally a product of all we were born with and all we have thought, said, done, and consumed since. We are the sum of our strengths, weaknesses, successes, and failures.

Similar to a fully developed tree branching beneath the sun, adulthood years are ripe with vitality and productivity. Our core bodies and minds are mature, but we also recreate ourselves with every passing year, like new flowers in springtime.

We devote ourselves to the hardships and fruits of family, work, and purpose. We become grounded responsible adults, hopefully valuing and happy with whom we've become. We discover that time is a commodity that causes conflict between our own wants and needs and the responsibilities of nurturing others.

The summer of this one life elapses, no longer by months and years, but somehow, by the decade. Then, one day, nature begins to change our chemistry again and we become aware that this vehicle, this body containing this being, is entering the next phase of life, middle adulthood, which I call gerolescence.

Gerolescence

What puberty lifted up, gravity pulls down.

As with adolescence, gerolescence can begin gradually or abruptly. Age fifty through seventy might seem a reasonable age range to ascribe as *gerolescent*, but even that's arbitrarily determined by social consensus. The onset of gerolescence might occur from a physical or social event, such as graying hair, retirement, or the birth of a grandchild.

Gerolescence is no less an opportunity than any other phase of life. While you still can, there's life to be lived: sights, sounds, smells, and tastes to be experienced and savored. By remembering our adolescent roots, we can unearth hidden strengths, forgotten talents, and simple joys. We can rediscover and revitalize the goodness of our youth and re-apply them to our later years. Recall what you did in youth to capture these sensorial delicacies and try to apply them now, somehow, some way.

Change, The Only Constant

Birth, aging, and death are nature's ways of reminding us that time flies. As we reach the middle and later decades, we're amazed that we get old so fast.

Whatever theory on aging—and why the body eventually exhausts itself—you subscribe to, the fact is, it does. Unlike the adolescent springtime of wild growth, gerolescence is an autumnal period preceding biological decline, and a chance to clean up the proverbial garden.

Gerolescence is puberty in reverse. Hormonal changes, for example, have a physical and psychological effect on seniors, altering their sexuality and secondary sexual characteristics. Endurance wanes, muscles tire, and joints creak. No organ system escapes the metabolic slowing caused by reduced resistance to gravity.

These don't have to be bleak anticipations. Attitude and physical disciplines are modifying factors; we have opportunity to prepare. Be grateful for these challenges. Without them, you'd be dead.

Identity

Old age is *showtime* after decades of rehearsal. During adolescence, identity formation occurs in relation to the surrounding adult environment. Then, as adults, we qualify ourselves by our work, family, and rank in a modern world. Our social attitudes and activities further represent our personal identities.

By the time we reach gerolescence, we've grown and shed aspects of our identities many times over. We usually know who and where we are in the history of the world. Gerolescence is the opportunity to take inventory of all those identities, with the goal of creating the next one.

Retirement is especially difficult for people who defer their personal ambitions and establish an identity based on external factors, such as professional or financial status. When fulfillment and identity have been predicated on a job title, some out-of-service seniors are not at all prepared to cope with their loss.

On the other hand, seniors who accept their gerolescent identities have an easier transition into the later years. They're willing and able to assume their roles as elders and more likely to continue contributing for the good of their peers and future generations.

While adolescents traditionally oppose the wisdom that comes from elders, functional gerolescents realize they have *become* the elders. Mature gerolescents listen—to others and to their own senses. Even though they may be met with resistance from those younger, seniors can recognize their roles in passing down to succeeding generations the history of life.

Hobbies, Talents, and Interests

What did you do for fun as a kid?

As mentioned, the demands of adulthood take much of our

time and we sometimes put to rest the interests from our youth. Adults learn to delay gratification as a reward for hard work. This may be a healthy work ethic. Often, however, people de-prioritize the responsibility of self-preservation and fail to relax adequately.

Maintaining pastime interests tends to promote acceptance and satisfaction with life. Leisure diversions help us be alone without feeling lonely. People who maintain personal interests seem better able to manage obstacles. Seniors who lack hobbies are among the most miserable.

How about playing a musical instrument? How about attending a community or sporting event, a collector's convention, a play, or a ballet? Would a set of old movies or symphonies, handcrafts, puzzles, a terrarium, a pet, or a short-wave radio be of interest? If you were a painter, a writer, or a potter, when was the last time you created something? Volunteer and meet people. Play cards. Take a class or go to a lecture.

I again emphasize that the key for maintaining active minds is communication and energy circulation. The brain needs to be exercised as much as the body that supplies it. Pursuing your interests offers not only purpose and satisfaction, but sometimes benefits others while creating social opportunities.

If you're stagnated and lack ideas, ask yourself, again, who is the child inside? What gave you some sense of happiness or gratification and what can you realistically do now to recreate or revisit some semblance of that enjoyment?

It's not too late to start now to maintain a diversity of interests for the rest of your life. A creative attitude can take you a long way.

Conflict and Conformity

Like adolescence, gerolescence is a time of revolution. Both age groups rebel against the elapsing of time, but the later years challenge our waning physical vitalities as well. In light of their approaching mortality, gerolescents may abandon some of society's conformities as they search for renewed fulfillment.

Gerolescence becomes a crossroads of personal discovery, when adults again question meaning and identity consistent with their stage of life. They examine choices and sacrifices made in the preceding years and accept the consequences of their commitments and deeds. Gerolescents assess their satisfaction and dissatisfaction with life.

It is truly healthy to take inventory of and validate middle-age desires and necessities. Mature resolutions are promoted from recognizing that adult yearnings probably parallel those of adolescence. Some react to gerolescence with a "midlife crisis." Anxiety that one's life is past its prime can lead to desperate attempts to recapture youth. Relationships, jobs, and responsibilities to oneself and others are sometimes compromised in an effort to relive the teenage years. Morals, values, and behaviors are subject to impulsivity or rampage.

But there are functional and dysfunctional ways to know happiness. In Chapter Six, I share a method for promoting success at meeting these and other challenges as we continue our journey through all the seasons of life.

Dealing With Gerolescence

The developmental phases of adolescence and gerolescence have many similarities, but they really are on opposite ends of the life spectrum. Keeping in mind that challenges are opportunities, the rest of this chapter identifies a few of the issues common among my middle- and late-life patients.

Stress

Stress, the energy created by opposing forces, is necessary for life. The pressure to survive (which has a lot to do with resisting gravity) increases with age.

Self-discipline may become more difficult, but engaging in certain behaviors and refraining from others are necessary to overcome distress and achieve goals. In gerolescence we have earned the right to labor and create with gratitude, simply for still being around to do so. Stressed by finite time, we stop asking for much. We seek less to impress others and instead to savor moments of earned pleasures.

Trauma

Childhood and adolescent hurts and traumas become a part of a person. Whether repressed or resolved, the wounds are biologically integrated into the soul.

Gerolescence affords the time to recognize and address issues of invalidation that may continue to compromise us. With wisdom comes the opportunity to no longer feel helpless about misfortunes or cruelties we were powerless against. Post-Traumatic Stress Disorder, as I wrote about earlier, matters at any age.

Metaphorically, trauma is the manure in life that can become fertilizer for growth. Quality aging sometimes requires a deliberate and maybe painful initiative to heal emotional wounds from adolescence. The reward for removing this psychological layer of "scar tissue" can include revealing the skills and attributes that were hidden behind the trauma.

Finances

Whether or not money is a root of evil, it signifies security for many elderly.

Financial stress can shorten lifespan. More and more seniors lack the funds necessary for maintaining independence and health. Monetary worries contribute to depression, avoidance of health care, and guilt over being a burden on others. Across the country, growing numbers of people are dependent on social services, but these resources are increasingly strained in their abilities to provide practical support.

Cognitively impaired seniors who have difficulty understanding finances are at the mercy of others. This situation is ripe for confusion, depletion, and exploitation. Those who lived through an impoverished childhood, such as the Great Depression of the 1930s, may still think milk and gasoline cost twenty-five cents a gallon. Denial can lead to paranoia, such as accusing intervening family, caregivers, and conservators of stealing. This is sometimes regarded as "punishing the rescuer."

Anticipating the future and preserving financial autonomy is best started in young adulthood. We need to communicate with trusted others and participate in self-discipline if we want to be provided for. Prevention is still the best intervention.

Divorce

Some people perceive their marriage and careers as stagnant. These issues are often valid and can sometimes be assertively resolved, but sometimes circumstances are what they are. In a divorce, family units are compromised, as are financial assets, living situations, and retirement savings.

Family loyalties are divided. The comfort years ahead are threatened. Unresolved anger can affect physical and mental health. Which kid takes care of mom and who's there for dad? My observation from working with seniors is too many divorced women, more so than men, lie in their nursing-home beds broke, angry, and alone.

Divorce is a type of death. To grow past this event, it helps to remember that relationships with nature, each other, and especially ourselves are vital for longevity. Many people in our personal, social, and vocational circles are dealing with their own gerolescence as we go through ours. That means there are plenty of occasions to reconnect.

ANGRRRR!

Anger is the emotion that most threatens a fulfilled gerolescence. Anger shortens lifespan by promoting illness. Accompanying anger are impatience, anxiety, and self-defeat, all variations on the experience of helplessness.

Anger includes beliefs of entitlement to benefits not earned. Gerolescents have weathered life, thus giving them ownership for their existence. "Assumed" reliance on others (entitlement), however, often leads to resentment when expectations aren't met.

Anger is a pestilence prevalent in the world of geriatrics: in courtrooms arguing family inheritances, in break rooms at health clinics, and in telephone calls to insurance companies.

Like most people, I learned when and how to get mad from the world around me. I learned by observing and practicing, and from my parents as taught to them by their parents. I have learned that I am the creator of my anger and its keeper.

As I will soon discuss, most people are capable of reducing anger by applying recognition and validation techniques to manage stressful situations to the best of their ability. Preemptively practicing self-discipline reduces anger, which translates to a more fruitful senescence and reduced risk of dementia.

We are powerless over aging and death; we are not helpless about living. Sometimes misfortunes are due to the forces of nature, another person, or one's own choices and actions. No one deserves to suffer, but it's usually up to us to earn our way out of hardship. Powerless is what we are in the face of destiny beyond our control. Helpless is when our outlook and attitude interfere with our ability to respond. When we understand the difference between being powerless and helpless, we can choose wisely.

Gravity

Gravity is at work throughout the universe. All life depends on it. It allows the Earth its firmament and the oceans their water. But it also causes us to bow down, like a tree branch weighted by heavy snow.

As long as we're able to physically resist gravity, to circulate blood and breathe air, we're alive. When we succumb to gravity's pull, we die. Dementia occurs when gravity is stronger than the body's ability to nourish the brain. The basic sugars, proteins, and fats become sluggish and form sediment in nerve tissues.

Neither a dandelion seed nor bird can float forever. All living things must eventually return to rest. Leaves fall.

Until then, move it or lose it.

Mortality

I will die. Maybe, as you're reading this book, I'm already gone. You too will die someday.

Getting older is the reward for staying alive. Most of us want this, provided our minds remain intact. The closer in years to death than birth, the more we appreciate how precious time and life are. We can accept mortality as we actively defy it. Not unlike an adolescent, a gerolescent seeks answers to the challenge: A quality life is more important than longevity. The elder, having additional years of experience, however, knows how potentially great one's contribution can be to the circle of nature.

Procrearticulation

As this chapter advances toward the conclusion of its own gerolescence, I again remind everyone of the talents, knowledge, and gifts each has to offer themselves and others. A tree in full bloom has about 250,000 leaves. I am convinced there are as many ways a person can express him or herself.

Procreation means to give birth, to create someone or something. Articulation is the ability to describe a thought or idea clearly. An artist expresses beauty through the procreation of a work of art. All gerolescents are artists.

The combination of these two words into the term "procrearticulation" describes a fundamental task of gerolescence: creating something good for the world as a way of appreciating and restituting what we've taken during our lifetime. The act of aging gracefully with health, creativity, and joy can be considered an art form in the sense that it emulates the vitality, beauty, and dignity of life.

Some goals are met in relation to our careers and communities; others are personal and spiritual. At various stages in growth we might aspire to be poets, teachers, athletes, scientists, musicians. Gerolescence offers the opportunity to *procrearticulate* a composition harvested from all our life's passions and experiences into a magnificent display of autumn foliage.

As long as we've got our senses, we are the authors of our life.

Shoveling Snow

I've been shoveling snow ever since I was a kid. I grew up in Illinois and we lived in a cul-de-sac at the bottom of a hill, surrounded by an abundance of woods and creeks nearby. A virtual winter wonderland.

We shoveled our own driveways and then we earned money shoveling for the neighbors. The elementary-school principal who

---

A Fable For The Ages

"The Hare darted almost out of sight at once, but soon stopped and, to show his contempt for the Tortoise, lay down to have a nap. The Tortoise plodded on and plodded on, and when the Hare awoke from his nap, he saw the Tortoise just near the winning-post and could not run up in time to save the race." —Aesop

I began acting more like a tortoise a few years ago. I realized I was like the rabbit, always racing around at work or on errands. Around age fifty, I realized where the race was heading, so I started darting less and plodding more.

In our formative years, we're often in a hurry with much to do and never enough time. In youth, life is a race whose finish line seems too far off in the distance to be truly appreciated. When I was younger, I probably scorned the tortoises that moseyed about, assuredly and unrushed. And then it occurred to me that like everybody else and without exception, I too was approaching my own inevitable winning-post.

Whenever I call to mind the tortoise, I start to slow down and assume a steadier pace. Being a tortoise requires deliberate action. I still pursue goals actively, work hard, and exercise, but I do so with a newfound respect for the moment. There is no need to fatigue myself, no rush to cross the finish line. I'll get there.

The youthful hares are welcome to pass me by. Elders can learn as much from the young as the young can from their elders. Besides, rabbits have a trait I admire: Nothing beats a good nap.

lived at the top of the street once paid my friend and me each with a bag of coins for shoveling her driveway and sidewalk. It seemed like a lot of money in those days—all those pennies, nickels, and dimes. The same day, we rode miles on our bicycles through the snow to the stores to buy snacks and comic books.

Sometimes after we finished the driveways, we kept on shoveling. We piled snow for sled jumps. We built snow forts with snow moats and snow chairs. We lay on our backs and looked up at the sky. Falling snow tickled our faces and tongues, flakes poking us gently in the eyes.

Forty years later, I'm still shoveling snow. The other night my children were outside with me, trudging pathways in the snow, building snow forts with snow chairs. We lay on our backs and let the snow fall on our faces.

Conclusion: Happiness

Since the springtime of your life, what pleasures have you earned that brought you happiness? What are the ingredients that brought you into being and sustained you throughout? What makes your spirit fly high?

We owe to the world and the universe much gratitude for having given us life. Surviving into old age takes effort, but it's worthwhile if done well. That's the essence of gerolescence. That's the nature of being okay with ourselves, of living life successfully, and of savoring moments.

Chapter Six

THE S.Wa.N.

Secure your own oxygen before assisting others.
—Airline advice

Swans are graceful and elegant birds. In mythology they symbolize power and transformation. As a cognitive-behavior therapy tool, the "S.Wa.N." is a technique I developed for promoting professional and personal empowerment and practical decision-making, thus a more gratifying life. Useful at any age and in any situation, the S.Wa.N. doesn't instruct *what* actions or behaviors to choose, but *how to choose them*. Either the S.Wa.N. has the potential to literally change your life or you already know how to do so.

As applied to aging and gerolescence, the S.Wa.N. helps us understand where we are and where we want, and need, to be. I've witnessed the transformative effect of the S.Wa.N. in my own life and in many others'. We better ourselves when we practice the disciplines needed to continue growing, season after season.

To master a talent you acquire and rehearse it. The ability to use and benefit from the S.Wa.N. is accomplished like any other skill: practice, practice, practice. Discipline requires effort; nothing worthwhile is easy. You certainly don't have to learn the S.Wa.N., but you might want to read this chapter with an open mind to determine if, in your opinion, it's a viable alternative to feeling helpless.

The Lesson

The S.Wa.N. is an acronym of three words: Should, Want, and Need. The definition of Should is "Other People's Opinion." The definition of Want is "My Opinion." The definition of Need is "Self-discipline To Achieve What I Want."

Should	"Other People's Opinion"
Want	"My Opinion"
Need	"Self-discipline To Achieve What I Want"

Repeat each word and its definition five times in a row, one term at a time. Consecutive repetition helps move immediately memorized data into long-range memory storage. Remember, practice leads to mastery:

Should	"Other People's Opinion"
Should	"Other People's Opinion"
Should	"Other People's Opinion"
Should	"Other People's Opinion"
Should	"Other People's Opinion"
Want	"My Opinion"
Want	"My Opinion"

Want	"My Opinion"
Want	"My Opinion"
Want	"My Opinion"

Need	"Self-discipline To Achieve What I Want"
Need	"Self-discipline To Achieve What I Want"
Need	"Self-discipline To Achieve What I Want"
Need	"Self-discipline To Achieve What I Want"
Need	"Self-discipline To Achieve What I Want"

Can you recite all three definitions without looking at the page?

Should

Other People's Opinions.

We begin receiving "should" messages before we're born: *I should feel the baby kicking in the womb.*

We hear them soon after birth: *The baby should be happy; I just fed and rocked him.*

As we grow older: *You should do your homework. You should get a job. You should marry. You should retire.*

Other people are always telling us *how we should live our lives.*

Should implies a mandate without choice. More examples include, "You should move your parents into your house." "You should be faithful to your partner." "You should get adequate rest and nourishment." It implies that you must, you have to.

Obviously, many people in this world hold different opinions about family and sexual morals; opinions abound as to what constitutes "adequate" rest and nutrition. You Need to do certain things if you Want certain outcomes. Do you want a job, a secure relationship, and good health?

To act because of a Should is to relinquish personal responsibility and behave based on the force or will of others. "Have to" and "ought to" (also known as "gotta" or "oughtta") are synonymous with Should. We don't *have to* bathe, eat, breathe, or treat other people respectfully. The consequences will be what they'll be, but we deceive ourselves when we state that we "should" do anything. There is nothing in life that we "have to" do except die someday.

Don't get me wrong. I seek and respect the opinions of others; I certainly live my life in consideration of Shoulds and I know they influence me. Ultimately, however, I reserve the right to make the final decision and bear the responsibility of the consequences.

The concept of Should is often regarded in therapy as a toxic word. Like the word "can't," both are regarded as self-defeating perceptions or attitudes. There are very specific behaviors that we "can't" do. I *can't* flap my arms and fly. I *can't* breathe underwater without supplemental oxygen. I *can't* understand the words when Bob Dylan sings. We *can't* defy the laws of physics.

"I can't" is more often used as a less-than-true excuse, implying "I'm not able." To say "I can't work two jobs," "I can't tell them no," or "I can't possibly do such-and-such" is often another way of saying, "I really don't want to" or "I don't need to."

The distinct difference between "I can't" and "I won't" can be significant in a clinical setting. Speech and physical therapists are among the allied health-care providers who can probably relate many anecdotes of capable clients who resist applying themselves because of psychological limitations. Similarly, part of my job is to consider what a patient Wants and try to facilitate what he or she Needs.

We often give in to the expectations that we Should have justifications and explanations in order to appease others, rather than ourselves. "I don't want to" is one of the most honest reasons and answers I know of.

By the time we reach gerolescence, we've had a lifetime of submitting to how we *should* live. We've also lived to some degree how we have *wanted* to. Each of us has the responsibility of fulfilling our wants and *needs*, but not at the expense of others; that's aggression, exploitation, and abuse. By recognizing and validating our individuality, we can take action for ourselves, then choose how we might help others.

If we want to care for someone else, it is responsible that we meet our own needs first. Self-preservation isn't selfishness. It's how we successfully get older. Adaptation is necessary if one wishes to thrive and grow, so old people must be doing something right.

When there's mastery of the Wants and Needs, there may be very few, if any, Shoulds.

Want

My Opinion.

This means I decide what and how I think, feel, and act. I might elicit input and then incorporate the opinions of others, but in the end, to the best of my ability, I am the owner of my behaviors. When I recognize and validate my own opinion, what I want, I assume responsibility for achieving my goals.

In other words, this is my life. What do I want to do with it?

Within the context of the S.Wa.N., please notice "Wa" is constructed with an upper-case **W** and a lower-case **a**. This is to emphasize that our Wants in life have different priorities and importance. We have BIG WANTS and small wants. Everyone is different, but valid less-important wants (and needs) include immediate pleasures and gratifications that make us feel good temporarily and contribute to long-term happiness. At other times we choose to exercise restraint or self-discipline, because the fulfillment from BIG WANTS in our opinion is more rewarding.

I might want a million dollars, but that's relatively small compared to the greater WANT of not engaging in illegal or unethical behaviors that compromise my health or integrity to acquire that million dollars (I neither want or need to go to prison).

Challenging is the situation where I Want to quit my employment, but I also Want a paycheck, so I Need to keep my job.

Need

A Self-discipline To Achieve What I Want.

I need oxygen, water, nutrition, and other vital necessities if I want to live (BIG WANT).

When driving my automobile, I stop at red lights because I need to, and not necessarily because I should. Maybe I don't want to, either. Theoretically, I'm in a hurry and I'm delusional about being more important than other motorists. I stop for the red light because I need to if I want not to hurt someone else or get a ticket.

In time, needs often become preferred wants. People who routinely exercise will agree they do so because they want to and actually feel a withdrawal of sorts when they don't. We can also experience withdrawal from the absence of intellectual challenges, sleep, and good nutrition.

Self-preservation is the balance between physical discipline and emotional reward. The application of the S.Wa.N. to the conflicts, challenges, and decisions in life is essentially this: Instead of asking yourself only what you should do (Other Peoples Opinions), ask yourself what you want to do (My Opinion), and what you think and feel you need to do (A Self-discipline To Achieve What

I Want). Recognize, then validate, your thoughts and feelings. Process what your head, heart, and gut intuitions are telling you.

Applying the S.Wa.N. enables you to conserve the energy previously spent on denial or rationalization. Instead, this method helps you focus, contemplate, and choose behaviors that lead to better outcomes for yourself, family, and patients.

Might

"Might" is full of *possibility*. Might is the antidote for the poisonous Shoulds in life. If Should is a toxin that sometimes paralyzes, Might is a strengthening remedy that resumes a person's control and flexibility. It offers protection against being helpless, even in a powerless situation. Might asserts itself against *should, can't, have to,* and *must*.

It's a pivotal word that promotes empowerment and choice. Might is a centered position, full of potential for movement and transformation.

Back to the examples of stopping at red lights, exercise, employment, or caring for seniors, I don't take action because I Should, but I Might need to if I Want a preferred outcome.

There are thousands of Should questions regarding geriatric health-care issues, such as medications, finances, guardianships, wills, living situations, relationships, restrictive interventions, rules and regulations, driving privileges, and other realities. Identify what the goals are and what available options *might* be implemented.

So, for quite a few of my patients' adult children who tell me, "I can't _____!" I validate and reassure their rights to act on their personal needs without feeling selfish or guilty. Worth repeating is that a person has the right to assume the responsibility for saying, "I don't want to," as the only explanation necessary.

I respond to their Should questions by examining Wants and
Needs, great and small. What are the personal, professional, and
moral goals for all involved parties? What might the options and
consequences be regarding every action and inaction? By avoiding
the Should approach to problem-solving and decision-making, prudent and practical interventions and outcomes are achieved.

Summarizing the S.Wa.N.

How Might you take responsibility for yourself first, and then
others? What would you Need to do to turn wishes into goals?
What are some of the Shoulds and shouldn'ts holding you back?

If you want not to feel angry or stagnated but instead be at
peace with yourself and personally empowered, what self-disciplines
might you need to practice? What actions might you choose to take
or not take, whether you want to or not, because there is something
greater that you seek? How might your remaining seasons be some
of the best?

SHOULD Other People's Opinion
WANT   My Opinion
NEED   Self-discipline to Achieve What I Want

Chapter Seven

LONGEVITY'S RAINBOW

A merry heart is a good medicine;
But a broken spirit drieth the bones.
—Proverbs 17:22

Time flies like an arrow; fruit flies like a banana.
—Groucho Marx

How magnificent it is that we live.

Ours is a world of diverse wonders, of beauty and pain, of joy and suffering. Life involves relishing moments and capturing as much enrichment as we can between birth and death, from the first leaf to the last flower.

We are capable of living longer while maintaining our senses and sensibilities. Many are fortunate to die with dignity.

There is an adage that "the sunset is no less spectacular than the sunrise." However, it seems to me that we can make the sunset even more glorious.

When it's finally our time, perhaps the hardest part of death isn't dying, but saying goodbye.

Anti Anti-Aging

"Anti-aging" health-care initiatives are generated by good intentions, but the "pro-longevity" movement has my vote. Anti-aging suggests resistance. Pro-longevity says keep going. Anti-aging has an aggressive implication. Pro-longevity encourages aging. You can't stop it, so why be against it?

Besides, I don't want to stop aging. I want to keep getting older for as long as I can. And I want to maintain my quality of life as I do.

Longevity is endurance. It's the Medal of Honor bestowed by Mother Nature. Getting older is not to be invalidated or resisted. As I wrote earlier, living a long time and making it worthwhile requires effort. We're entitled to nothing. We must earn old age and with it health, be it physical, spiritual, mental, financial, or otherwise.

Longevity is meaningless without purpose. A full bladder might get us out of bed in the morning, but we need a good reason to stay out of bed. Activities become more difficult in later years, but the alternative is stagnation, a condition that's lower than plant life.

Pro-longevity is a lifelong commitment. It begins as a thought and becomes an attitude, which can then translate into action. Together pro-longevity followers can create a movement. Anti anti-aging believers unite!

The Greatest Attitude

How we deal with life depends in part on our attitudes. Attitude is what differentiates our obstacles from our opportunities.

It determines whether we're empowered or helpless, whether we respond to situations as threats or as challenges.

Our frame of mind greatly affects our health. A positive attitude helps prevent illness and accelerates recovery when we do fall ill.

Perhaps the greatest attitude is gratitude. By being appreciative and not taking life for granted, we enhance our daily living. People practice gratitude in various ways. Some do so by sharing food, money, or time to help others. Some also express their gratitude through prayer or meditation.

No matter how gratefulness is felt or expressed, it's a discipline that, when practiced, reminds us of the humble joy of being mindful and living in the moment.

Birthdays

Birthdays evoke all kinds of reactions. Some people rejoice. Others don't want to acknowledge their own milestones. I have a friend who has celebrated his 39th birthday for the past fifteen years. I know others who abhor the thought of another year gone by. Others dismiss the occasion as "no big deal," yet they silently fume if nobody acknowledges the occasion. Still, wisdom dictates that passing another birthday is better than the alternative.

Birthdays are somewhat arbitrary anniversaries. Every day can be cause for celebration. I respect birthdays as a tradition or a ritual. Traditions are important opportunities for reminding us to pause and reflect. A birthday can be about gratitude. It's not about the presents received, for life itself is a gift. (It is, however, about the cake, but only if it's chocolate.)

Perhaps I have crossed the equatorial line of my lifespan. I celebrate the fact that fifty-two years ago, I took my first breath. How many more breaths will I be fortunate to experience before gravity causes my final exhalation?

I'm pleased to claim, with gratitude and humility, that I'm over 18,980 days old, yet I don't feel a day over 18,254.

The Discipline of Work and Play

As is written universally, the common denominator for success is discipline. Discipline means training a behavior in order to achieve a specific outcome. Healthy or not, the more we practice an action, the better we become at it

Discipline is not to be confused with aggression or forcing your will on other people. It's self-control with mindfulness, deliberately and confidently.

When we care enough, we discipline ourselves to exercise our bodies and minds to function optimally. A long life might be achieved with luck, but as the best gamblers know, the more disciplined you are, the luckier you'll be. Besides, "luck" is sweeter when it's achieved through discipline.

Two disciplines in particular promote healthy aging: labor and laughter.

Labor means to toil. Like all living organisms, people accumulate and expend energy, whether mental or physical, in order to exist. When work has significance, so does life. Labor is more than having a job; it's participating with the world for a purpose: the benefit of oneself, others, or both.

Joy, like sunshine, is also a necessary discipline for enhanced growth. As I've said, I believe that happiness is achieved by earning moments and pleasures. When labor and laughter are engaged, the body and brain are invigorated and so is life. Participate in activities that matter to you, even if you sometimes have to force yourself.

Remember that there's always work to be done, and laughter sweetens the labor.

Retirement

"A goal without a plan is just a wish."
—Antoine St. Exupré

There comes a time in life when most people make a significant accommodation for their later years and stop working formally. This is called "retirement." But retirement can be the opposite: a time for re-employed energies with a purpose.

Retirement is a time for discovery and new experiences. We can travel by land, sea, or air. We can also travel socially, emotionally, and spiritually. We can even travel in our imagination through any dimension of time or space, without having to leave our favorite chair: simply by reading a book or watching a movie.

Retirement from the labor force in no way implies that life's work is complete. On the contrary, it's a time to adjust behavior in preparation for the proverbial road ahead. To make your journey as long and rewarding as is practical, keep your body and mind as mobile as possible. With a new set of life "treads," we're ready to move forward. What a glorious challenge and opportunity!

Words From The Wise

I have a 91-year-old client who has a 68-year-old daughter. Both are reasonably healthy and both are coping with various changes in their health and lifestyles.

Mother and daughter represent a significant demographic in today's America: seniors caring for seniors. The daughter also embodies the phenomenon of the "sandwich generation," where middle-aged adults care for their elderly parents and their own younger children.

These two ladies are fortunate in that they've maintained healthy relationships throughout their lives and are able to live near each other in the same town. They've achieved a balance between caring for immediate and extended family and finding time to care for themselves.

According to the mother, her longevity is attributed to good genes and not taking a lot of medication. She cited feeling "lucky to be here" and laughed that she remains "one day ahead of death."

She recently relinquished the privilege of driving. She accepted that her risk of being involved in an accident had become too great. She feels a loss of the freedom that driving once allowed.

The daughter encourages her mother and other seniors to "get out, adapt, and take advantage of social-interaction opportunities." She cautions against watching too much television, which isolates people and dulls the senses.

They both agree that "living right" includes healthy exercise and diet, and meaningful activities before and during one's elderhood.

I am grateful to share the wisdom of these two instructive women. As I have complimented many of my elderly clients, "You might not be a spring chicken, but you're not ready yet to be the Thanksgiving turkey!"

Six Ways to Expedite Personal Decline

1. *Don't Exercise.* Regardless of your state of health, the number-one factor for promoting longevity with quality is exercise. So by all means, never challenge yourself physically, mentally, spiritually, or socially. The less you exert yourself, the quicker your well-being will decline and the more miserable you'll be.

2. Eat More Junk Food. Fried foods from the drive-through window and sweets from the bakery are especially effective for invalidating your body's nutritional needs. And don't just limit yourself to three meals a day, either. Grazing day and night is what fattening foods are for.

3. Isolate Yourself. You've worked hard all your life to secure your own little corner. Limiting your interactions with other people is a great way to lose touch with yourself and the world around you. And why not? The television can keep you company.

4. Over-medicate. Unless you're on medications for your heart, breathing, digestion, pain, appetite, mood, memory, sleep, bladder, tremors, and more, ask yourself, "Am I keeping up with America's obsession with pills?" Do your part. If you're not exceeding the minimal necessary number of medications your body can tolerate, the pharmaceutical industry won't be able to continue draining valuable health-care dollars that could be applied to much greater use.

5. Act Entitled. After raising a family, saving money, contributing to charity, working, and paying your dues to society, it's time to sit back and let others take care of you. Why bother doing anything for yourself? Vegetating in your retirement years is a sure-fire method for allowing gravity to pull you ever closer to the ground.

6. Drink and Smoke. Smoking does its best damage when enjoyed before, during, or after you take your breathing medications. Similarly, excessive alcohol is a terrific way to counteract the efforts of any health initiatives. Drinking in the evening is an excellent way to compromise sleep, aggravate depression, and increase irritability. Better yet, tell yourself you're a connoisseur and you can drink as much as you want.

Good luck!

The Rule of Least Restriction

Living independently and making our own decisions are at the core of personal freedom. However, when a person fails to thrive, restrictive interventions may become appropriate. I'm often asked to assess whether someone's life would be better off as a result of reduced rights (see Chapter Eight).

Interventions can partially or completely remove the decision-making rights of an individual, which is why the Rule of Least Restriction is a reminder to intervene in another person's life *as little as necessary*. This guideline applies medically, physically, and chemically, but also financially, socially, and spiritually.

The rule, as it applies to medical interventions, refers to information sharing, hospitalization, invasive procedures, surgeries, and medications, and their physical, emotional, and financial costs.

Behavior problems present challenges for implementing least-restrictive intervention guidelines. For example, are drugs more or less restrictive than physical restraint? It depends on circumstances. Medicating is highly controversial as a form of chemical intrusion for agitated dementia patients. Abiding by the Rule of Least Restriction includes minimizing the use of mind-altering medications and physical enclosure in amounts and duration, and acknowledges the rights and responsibilities involved with stopping the misbehavior.

The Rule of Least Restriction also applies when making living wills, powers of attorney, and trusts, as well as guardianship and conservator determinations.

Removing a driver's license symbolizes restriction of freedom and can be a significant loss to an older person. Rebellion against restricted driving, combined with the poor judgment of doing so anyway, adds to risk.

More invasive is removing a senior from his or her own private residence. Even when it's warranted and consented, leaving one's home can have serious consequences, including the loss of the will to live.

These examples illustrate some of the psychological consequences of removing a person's integrities. That's why sometimes, ironically, so many social-service, legal, and health professionals get involved: to ethically assure the patient's needs are best protected using the least restrictive means.

Non-Pharmacologic Interventions

In the spirit of interfering as little as necessary, we prefer the most natural interventions as possible using the least amount of prescription drugs. Non-pharmacologic interventions require a good team of people, a positive and safe environment, and a lot of other resources, not the least of which are time and compassion. Mood- and behavior-modifying medications are overused in place of patient (and caregiver) holistic support.

Engaging the senses through gardening, exercise and yoga, music, games, pet and craft therapy, nutrition, massage, and aromatherapy stimulates to some degree even those with advanced stages of dementia.

Group and peer support is recognized as another essential component, offering attention to patients, as well as validation for their caregivers who wish to avoid burnout.

Non-pharmacologic interventions often require creativity and seemingly more resources than medication management for dementia-related problems, but successful outcomes are usually more cost-effective and humanely superior.

Swimming In the Ocean of Life

Dementia can be likened to swimming in the middle of the ocean. You're surrounded by water with no shore in sight. You swim and paddle about to keep afloat, but with dementia you feel lost and, perhaps, panicked. You could drown out there.

When the ocean of life becomes too overwhelming, it's sometimes appropriate to provide the lost "swimmer" a smaller environment with secured boundaries. A swimming pool, for example, has sides to hold onto and a bottom to stand on. In a swimming pool, even a "non-swimmer" can skillfully splash about with a sense of dignity and security.

It's responsible to provide people who have dementia the least confining living situation, when practical. To those of us who still possess clear thinking and reason, the idea of senior-living facilities may seem like warehouses, cages, or mausoleums. To the cognitively impoverished, however, they are tranquil waters that shelter them from the storm.

Cadillac Care For Volkswagen Prices

Americans are living longer and ever-greater demands are being placed upon extended-care facilities (ECFs). As someone who spends long hours in nursing homes, I'm grateful to those who work in them, caring for the infirm and the elderly.

Most extended-care facilities aren't luxurious. They do their best to provide reasonable care with the resources they have. The staff-to-patient ratios are often misproportioned; funding and salaries are limited. Not only must standards of care be maintained, but the demands of the patients, administrators, and families must be satisfied.

People have to be fed and cleaned, medications need to be dispensed, therapies provided, and telephone calls answered. Everything is supposed to be documented. Staffs have also to chaperone government and corporate visitors, attend mandatory meetings, address sudden mishaps, and explain to family visitors why a pill or a bath hadn't been given "on time."

The medical and legal costs of increased longevity are straining resources. Americans are saving less money, while government and pension resources are becoming less reliable. Bad habits, poor nutrition, and obesity are epidemic in a nation that feels entitled to quality health care.

ECFs continue to serve people unable to take care of themselves. The growth in demand for long-term care is outpacing the capacity to provide. And yet, the workers show up and keep these facilities running twenty-four hours a day, seven days a week, including holidays.

My Four Songs

Four of my favorite songs are "Moon River" (Mancini), "The Swan" (St. Saens), "Laudate Dominum" (Mozart), and "Cavatina" (Myers). I have these four songs recorded on one CD. I've requested that they be played at my funeral.

Plenty of people are uncomfortable addressing end-of-life issues. Many haven't prepared wills, trusts, burial or other directives for the event of their death. It's too morbid or premature; some people simply don't know how or where to begin.

Fortunately, if you're reading this, you have now been around long enough to know better. Assume nothing.

Why not prepare your own party? We celebrate birthdays, anniversaries, and retirement. We can at least indicate what we might or might not want for our own sendoff.

My song choices have changed over the years to reflect my life. I plan to live for a very long time. However, if I want to have specific music played at my service, that's up to me. After all, as the saying goes, it's my funeral.

Chapter Eight

ASSESSING DEMENTIA

A physician is obligated to consider more than a diseased organ, more even than the whole man—he must view the man in his world.
—Harvey Cushing

The bodies of seed plants consist of roots, stems, and leaves.
—College Botany

In medical school I was taught to promote health, healing, and comfort. I took an oath to do no harm.

I received instruction through teachers, books, lectures and laboratories, and patients. I watched and listened, and I pledged to apply my knowledge to helping others.

I learned about the genesis and exodus of life: conception and the birth process, the developmental stages, health and disease, and dying. I was fortunate to be disciplined *how* to think, and not just *what* to think.

The medical field has gained tremendous insight about the mysteries of life, aging, and longevity. Yet our knowledge is modest about a universe too vast for us to fully comprehend. Doctors today must acquire a knowledge base, applying what they do know and respecting what they *don't* know.

Managing the health declines of an aging population requires team coordination, utilizing conventional and alternative health-care providers and proper methods. The doctors who practice geriatric medicine come from specialties including internal medicine, family practice, neurology, and psychiatry. Many practitioners specialize in diagnosing and treating cognitive declines, and yet there is a shortage.

I've discovered that the challenges of managing dementia and promoting life with quality require not only medical knowledge, but also common sense and ethics. To this end, all physicians treating all patients carry the responsibilities of leadership in the understanding of and caring for those who suffer.

Nursing Home Consultation

Mrs. Flora is a single elderly female who, prior to admission to the Lucky Star senior nursing facility, was living independently in her own home. She tended not to drink enough water, because she didn't want to urinate even more frequently then she already was. She started to feel unwell, so she shakily drove to an urgent-care clinic and was prescribed an antibiotic for a bladder infection. From the antibiotic she experienced nausea, reduced appetite, and loose bowels. She was then prescribed medication to stop the diarrhea.

In a short time, however, Mrs. Flora noticed her throat and mouth were drier and she'd become more constipated than ever before. Her fluid and nutritional imbalance, combined with her medications, started

to cause dizziness and heartbeat irregularity. She was referred to a car-
diologist who prescribed a heart medication or two and soon Mrs. Flora
became tremulous and less coordinated. A consultation with a neurolo-
gist resulted in her getting more medications and she became forgetful,
irritable, and confused.

Next, a well-meaning nurse practitioner prescribed memory
stabilizers and a sedative for nervousness. For Mrs. Flora's erratic
bowel functions with reduced appetite and weight, the gastroenterologist
recommended an endoscopy. A gastric-acid reflux suppressant and an
appetite-promoting agent were added to her drug regimen.

During the endoscopy procedure, Mrs. Flora was sedated and
experienced a transient reduction in oxygenation and blood pressure.
Afterwards, narcotics and sedatives were administered to relieve pain
and promote rest.

At the hospital, a psychiatrist was consulted, because Mrs. Flora
acted depressed and thought disorganized. A cognitive assessment
resulted in more diagnoses and some antidepressant and antipsychotic
medications.

Mrs. Flora had now been diagnosed as having Alzheimer's Dementia with Behavioral Problems (along with urinary-tract infection, dehydration and electrolyte imbalance, cardiac arrhythmia, encephalopathy,
gastric-esophageal reflux disease, and major depression with psychosis).
Specialists had prescribed more than a dozen medications.

Mrs. Flora became the parts of her sum.

A portion of my consultation and assessment was to consider
her original complaint. What caused her urinary-tract infection?
What were her original needs? How could the dozen medications
be tapered? Was a nursing home necessary?

Cognitive and mood problems, delirium, and dementia are not

uncommon consequences of specialty care. I've known far too many patients whose medical treatments or surgeries were "successful," but whose minds and spirits were compromised.

Labels

Anyone can become aggressive and psychotic while delirious from an acute medical illness. I have consulted on patients who were paranoid and agitated from urinary-tract infections that progressed to body-wide infection with delirium. When the infections are resolved, the violent behaviors cease.

This not-uncommon situation can lead to the diagnosis "Dementia with Behavior Disturbance." These patients are now "labeled" and their treatment and dispositions could be forever compromised.

Labeling can create a false reputation that precedes the individual. A single convulsion does not automatically mean a seizure disorder. An episode of hallucinating isn't necessarily schizophrenia. Medication delirium is not Alzheimer's Dementia.

The Patient Is A Person

Biology is the study of organisms in their environments. Disease states may be similar from patient to patient, but no two people or set of circumstances are exactly alike. Comprehensive diagnosis and treatment of someone who is anxious, delirious, demented, and can't function on his own needs to consider the countless ways in which patients are unique human organisms in their unique environments with their unique histories.

A mentor taught me to approach a patient as if this were my own mother, father, or sibling (the instructor assumed I liked my family!). How might I want my relations, or even myself, to be managed if the tables were turned?

Who's Being Treated Here?

Sometimes we treat the illness, sometimes the person, and sometimes the situation. At times, finances and insurance, or government and health-care regulations, influence treatment. Caregivers and family members also weigh in on decisions and treatment. Every person and provider has his or her own set of philosophies, ethics, and expectations. The feelings and attitudes of everyone involved, consciously or unconsciously, directly or indirectly, all factor into a patient's treatment.

Honest treatment is meant to promote healing by relieving suffering and improving the quality of a person's life. Intuition, experience, open-mindedness, and knowledge on the part of all concerned parties lead to treatment in the *patient's* best interest. Sometimes, although I'll validate what a person may *want*, I'm obligated to enhance what the patient *needs*.

So Many Questions

Literally, thousands of questions can be asked regarding health and wellness. Issues of mood, sleep, appetite, energy, and motivation are pertinent. Further inquiries can be made into memory, sight, hearing, touch, joint and muscle aches, chest pain, headaches, or bowel and bladder functions. Difficulties with breathing, walking, and medications are also considered. Hours can be spent.

A patient, especially elderly and of limited endurance, will tolerate only so much interrogation. A clinical assessment by necessity must consist of a finite number of questions. This in itself is a piece of the evaluation puzzle: You can ask *anything*, but you can't ask *every*thing.

I try to ask questions that elicit the best information and give clues to the next best question.

One O'Clock Office Patient

I greet and ask Mr. Castleman why he's seeing me, and how I might be of help to him.

"Can you hear me all right? How are you feeling?"

I then ask more specifically about his physical comfort, and whether he's calm, depressed, confused, or anxious. I ask him about his energy, sleep, appetite and bodily functions, self-esteem, and, perhaps, libido.

"How are you getting by from day to day? Are you bored?"

I ask if he's been tearful or angry lately and about his attitudes on life and living. I inquire about anxiety and mood swings by asking if has obsessions, compulsions, or fears. I ask about substance use.

I inquire about his memory and concentration. Has forgetfulness resulted in dangerous or distressed situations, such as a pan burning on the stove, bath water overflowing, or utilities being turned off for bill non-payment?

I ask Mr. Castleman about his thoughts, if they make sense. Are they calm, restless, or distressful? I ask about his mental-health history and his family's alcohol, mental-health, and dementia history. I ask him to recall some of his childhood and adulthood memories and about past and present hobbies and goals.

I ask Mr. Castleman his date of birth, age, relationship history, and current family status. I ask what his vocation was, his current living circumstances and support systems, and his spiritual preference. "What are your pastimes and what do you look forward to?"

Medical-history inquiries include medical illnesses, medications and allergies, surgeries, and how he perceives his health condition is. If medical reports, laboratory values, and medication lists are available, I include them in my appraisal.

I've meanwhile been formally assessing his emotional, behavioral, and thinking processes, while observing his appearance and behaviors. I notice his eye contact, speech, and other communication abilities. I test his motor skills and give him questions involving math, grammar, memory, and problem solving. I assess his orientation, mood, and awareness of his situation. I estimate if he's suicidal or paranoid. All the while I'm listening, watching, thinking, and feeling my intuitions.

"Mr. Castleman, this is what I think your medical, cognitive, and psychological situation is," I tell him, in a way that he can understand and cope with. We discuss our mutual opinions, treatments options, his preferences, and their risks and benefits. I assess to the best of my ability what Mr. Castleman wants and needs, and design a realistic responsible plan.

Dandelion Medicine

Dandelions are weeds, but they're also flowers and plants. I was taught that a "weed" has no known benefit, but becomes regarded as a "plant" once its properties are discovered. Dandelions can be considered a nuisance or be appreciated for their beauty. People have used dandelions for medicinal value; others enjoy it as a wine.

When asked to imagine or draw a dandelion, most people visualize a flower, leaves, and a stem. These are the visible parts. To understand a dandelion in its entirety, however, means that the roots must also be represented.

I use the concept of "dandelion medicine" as a metaphor for how modern medicine is often practiced. Too frequently, we address and treat only the visible part of the problem.

To seek only relief from symptoms is to risk ignoring the root cause of a problem. Specialists are often successful at stabilizing situations without fully recognizing, addressing, and resolving the underlying issues. As with any "weed," if you don't eradicate the roots, the problem grows back again.

If your garden of life has been around long enough, then you've likely encountered other weeds before. For someone to be old enough to develop dementia usually requires a once reasonably hearty garden. Perhaps dementia, like an unidentified weed, has properties not readily recognized as beneficial, a possibility touched on earlier in this book.

Environmental exposures, what we put in the soil, and how we nurture our garden all determine our vulnerability to life's weeds. Choices made during the preceding decades are forerunners of health, or the lack thereof, in later years. A garden is never complete; it requires ongoing cultivation or it will die.

The metaphor of dementia as a weed helps you understand its underlying causes and progression. It illustrates some of the successes and limitations in treating dementia and other aging challenges. You can visualize how dementia's roots, literally and figuratively, might spread and choke out the healthy garden of a thinking mind.

Identifying the source of any medical dysfunction is like appreciating a dandelion's roots. For example, Mrs. Flora's dizziness was the visible aspect of her core problems. Recognizing and correcting the medication side effects and underlying imbalances in fluids and body salts may have been a less restrictive intervention than adding more drugs.

The dementia expert knows that dementia is a result of physiological imbalances inside and outside the central nervous system. Hypertension, lung disease, diabetes, renal failure, and disorders of gastrointestinal, blood, hormone, bone, muscle, fluid, and electrolyte systems can singularly or collectively challenge brain function.

The basic objective of the cognitive evaluation is to determine a patient's limits of memory, thought processing and knowledge, and reasoning ability. Beyond that, the evaluator sets and helps actuate goals. Once these steps are accomplished, the interventions appropriate to the patient's condition are implemented.

My job is to assess, diagnose, and treat signs and symptoms. A sign is an objective finding on the part of the health provider. A symptom is a subjective complaint expressed by the patient or his/her representative. For example, my child might complain of the symptom of having a sore throat; a reddened swollen tonsil is a sign of tonsillitis.

I continually remind myself that a dementia assessment is a many-rooted biopsychosocial evaluation. When opportunity allows, a complete cognitive assessment includes physical findings, along with historical and current medical, psychological, and social information.

Some medical histories may never be unearthed. Genetics and gestation, for example, or birth and perinatal events might have a lifetime impact; however, this kind of developmental information might never get discovered, especially seventy or eighty years later.

Ultimately, there are many factors to consider when completing the picture of the dandelion dementia, its roots and environment. We now create an opportunity for doing something about it, practically and with integrity.

Assessing the Patient

Assessing Oneself

Before we can assess someone else, we need to assess ourselves.

We begin the appraisal of our own mental state every day the moment we awaken. As we gain consciousness and our senses become alert, we orient ourselves in time and space. We register our comforts and pains, physically and mentally.

Many of us begin the day standing in front of the bathroom mirror; a picture is worth a thousand words. We register our appearance, odor, mental clarity, and psychological well-being. We gauge ourselves and go out into the day.

The fundamental tools for performing a mental-status assessment exist within our own senses. We look, we smell, and we listen. We also receive information through touch and skin responses, such as chills or goose bumps. We think with our minds, feel with our hearts, and listen to the intuitions provided by our "gut feelings."

Medical expertise requires knowledge and intuition. Additional standardized testing provides objective validation that qualifies and quantifies the clinical experience, but you don't have to be a doctor to know when someone is sick. Often, we ourselves remain the best diagnostic instrument for assessing the physical and mental states of older adults.

Surveying the Situation

I was taught that a medical consultation begins with a question. A concern about an older patient arises that seeks to be resolved and an assessment of her mental-health status is launched. Some of the potentially endless questions related to assessing cognitive function and dementia are as follows:

Why has an assessment been requested and why at this particular time?

Is this an emergency, urgency, or an elective intervention?

Who's requesting the assessment and who's being evaluated?

Who arranges the evaluation and coordinates the resources?

What are the specific questions to be answered and problems to be addressed?

What methods of assessment will be utilized? How and where will information be communicated before, during, and after the assessment is completed?

When and where will the assessment take place and when will the results be known?

When can the recommendations be implemented?

How will the assessment impact the individual, the family, and the community?

The Subjective History

The Chief Complaint

The chief complaint is medical terminology for the primary reason a patient is being treated. Common chief complaints might include headache, poor sleep and fatigue, ringing ears, pain, depression, or forgetfulness. Often, the evaluation of cognitively impaired seniors is requested by outside referral sources, but it's still part of the assessment process to ascertain the patient's perspective for being in a medical or care-receiving situation.

Review of Systems

When practical, the patient is asked to elicit his perception of whether he has emotional or cognitive difficulties, physical health concerns, or particular psychosocial stressors. These inquiries provide the evaluator an insight into the subjective needs of the patient and help direct the interview's focus.

Substance History

Aging bodies grow less tolerant of exposure to substance use and abuse. The implications of the use of psychoactive agents range from insignificant to life-threatening.

Virtually any drug has a risk of adverse effects. Depending on the evaluation's circumstances, my inquiries might focus on exposures to legal agents such as caffeine, tobacco, over-the-counter (OTC) and prescription medications, alternative and supplemental health-care agents, and illicit drugs.

Alcohol use can be obvious or hidden, innocent or extreme, beneficial or deadly. An alcohol-history evaluation can be initially brief, then expanded as necessary, but it's vital for a complete dementia assessment. I have too often read cognitive assessments that don't even mention alcohol, yet this issue is widespread among the young and elderly. In addition, its effects are further aggravated when a patient also takes a number of prescription and OTC medications. Alcohol, in combination with health declines and depression, becomes increasingly lethal.

The Stress List

Sometimes I help my cognitively intact patients make a list of their current stressors. Commonly, issues that cause stress in elderly include finances, relationships and family, health problems, and attitudes about aging, purpose, and meaning.

Stress is neither good nor bad until it's put in a context that relates to one's quality of life. Although a reported distress may not be reality-based, it can be real to the believer. Some people deny having stressors at all; others may report feeling overwhelmed.

As reviewed earlier, patients who are aware that they're losing their cognitive faculties can be additionally stressed. It's difficult to observe one's self losing the ability to manage life independently, forfeit possessions and autonomy, and consequently relinquish integrity and control to others.

Those with more advanced dementia are sometimes less distressed, consistent with a comfortable obliviousness. Sometimes it is relevant for me to assess the stress of the accompanying family member.

Medical History

A patient's medical history identifies acute and chronic illnesses, medications, and allergies, as well as past traumas, illnesses, and surgeries. Cognitive disorders almost always have traceable roots to medical conditions that often include diabetes, lung and heart disease, or hypertension.

Sometimes patients aren't keen on knowingly being assessed for their cognition, mood, and intellect. Justifiably, people defend their mental integrities. Earlier, I stated that I might start my interview with a general question about "physical" and not "mental" health issues. This way I establish a medical atmosphere before prying into their psyche.

NKDA (No Known Drug Allergies)

A medication allergy means that the body has a significantly adverse reaction to a particular drug. If severe enough, a person can go into cardiovascular or pulmonary shock. Less severe reactions may include rashes, swelling, itching, or joint pain.

An allergy is different than an adversity, which includes exaggerated responses such as over-sedation or paradoxical reactions that occur opposite of the expected intent. Undesired responses to drugs are legitimate, but it's important to distinguish these terms to avoid erroneous information in a patient's file.

A long list of medication allergies sometimes suggests a heavily medicated past. I might enquire, "Why has she been exposed to so many medications? Why have so many of them been pain-related or psychoactive substances?"

Medication Profile

It is my clinical experience that an assessor's awareness about heart and water pills, liver and cholesterol pills, bladder and bowel pills, breathing pills, pain pills, muscle relaxants, sleeping pills, and all the other neurologic and psychiatric medication relationships cannot be overly emphasized. Medications have become one of the primary factors influencing cognitive and functional disabilities among seniors.

Questions about current drugs being used are concerned with the reasons for taking them, dosages and frequencies, how long they've been used, or how long since they were last used. Sometimes it matters knowing about previous medications, why they were used, and why and when they were discontinued.

Practitioners know we won't always get a complete medication history. Perhaps medications were stopped, forgotten, or duplicated due to impaired memory. Or maybe refills ran out months ago, but the patient discovered an old bottle of something "similar" and took extra pills to compensate.

Medical Illness History

A patient's diagnostic profile is a list of all past and present illnesses and any significant recurrences. Multiple medical problems increase the risk of depression and cognitive declines in later years.

As I've said, only so many questions can be asked about so many body parts. A clinical review might start with global questions about the heart, lung, kidney, and digestive systems. Infections, cancer, diabetic and thyroid problems, along with bowel and bladder difficulties, are relevant to ask about, because of their common co-occurrences with dementia.

"Noggin" and Trauma History

The medical fields of neurology and psychiatry overlap; i.e., they both focus on the brain. Psychiatrists need a working knowledge of neurology and vice versa. As part of the neurocognitive assessment, I ask patients about their neurological histories. Strokes, transient ischemic attacks (TIAs), loss of consciousness, seizures, tremors, dyscoordination, weakness, pain, headaches, difficulty swallowing, and declines in taste, touch, sight, hearing, and smell are some of the many neuropsychiatric events that affect mental functioning.

The dementia evaluator also gains by knowing of any relevant head or facial traumas that may predispose a person to dementia. I once met Jacob in a long-term locked-ward facility, whose diagnosis of "Alzheimer's-type Dementia, advanced stage, with behavioral disturbance" I believed to be inaccurate. When I was the first to question the family if he'd had a trauma history, they recalled Jacob's two automobile mishaps a few years prior to the onset of his cognitive decline. In one, he slammed his forehead against the windshield; the second accident fractured his nose on the steering wheel.

Jacob's frontal-brain trauma and low oxygen due to his deviated nasal passage were prominent contributions to his dementia. His outbursts had become so violent that they were resistant to potent medications used for behavior and thought stabilization without giving rise to more serious medical problems. Jacob had to be transferred to a unit appropriate for his rapidly accelerating decline.

Respiratory History

The above example illustrates why my dementia questions include uncovering airway obstructions and anatomical blockages (such as a deviated nasal septum), sinusitis or seasonal allergies, or enlarged tongues and tonsils. As I discussed in the chapter on sleep and dementia, I want to know if patients have had nose or jaw fractures or trauma, incurred perhaps from fights, childhood mishaps, or athletic events. These are significant data that can explain a lot of sleep, behavior, and concentration problems.

Asthma, emphysema, and environmental allergens and toxins can all lead me to consider a history of oxygen deprivation. I've known patients who were affected by agricultural pesticides, nitroglycerin, and cigarette smoking. One of my patients suffered memory problems related to a restrictive lung disease resulting from childhood exposures to toxic chemicals in his family's dry-cleaning shop.

I also evaluated a patient who had worked for decades at a renowned amusement park as a maintenance engineer. His responsibilities included removing paint from and repainting rides and attractions. He eventually developed a respiratory disease after a career of breathing noxious aerosols, which I believe was a fundamental cause of his dementia condition known as encephalomalacia. His brain had "softened" by definition, as the nerves cells died from chemical toxicity. My recommendations to assist this man's case were to reduce medications I thought were exacerbating his restlessness, and a trial of supplemental oxygen.

Surgical History

Surgery often affects the entire body, not just the specific organ. Surgery is life-saving, but involves sedation, perhaps mechanical ventilator support, and sometimes heart machines. The deeper the anesthesia, the more vulnerable the body is to oxygen compromise.

Surgical events can cause cognitive losses. The nervous system can tolerate only so much oxygen starvation. Multiple surgeries throughout a lifetime, along with the use of post-operative sedatives and pain relievers, can accumulate and predispose people to dementia and other neuropsychiatric dysfunction.

Developmental History

Information about an older patient's childhood and life history can sometimes be a goldmine of treatment resources. This line of inquiry is meant to unearth relevant information about adolescent and adult experiences and attitudes that contribute to the person's current makeup. For me, the developmental history establishes the cornerstone of Gerolescence, as elaborated earlier.

Because this portion of the assessment contains so many "roots," I wait until after eliciting the medical history, hoping to have gained trust and a conversational ambience. I start this part of the evaluation by asking seniors to tell me in a few words about their childhoods. Their summaries reveal essentials about their personality development.

I try to remain sensitive when I question childhood traumas or disabilities, so I don't evoke undue distress. When I was in medical school, a surgeon taught me, "Don't open what you can't close."

I might ask Mr. Kowalski about the environments and milestones in his life, from birth until the present. I inquire of career, relationship, legal, financial, military, and spiritual experiences. I ask about his accomplishments, regrets, hobbies, and goals.

If Mr. Kowalski had any musical, athletic, or intellectual interests during childhood and beyond, this too is worthwhile information for psychosocial treatment planning. Dormant passions from the past can stimulate ideas for current activities. An older adult may not have the physical ability to engage in the rigors of youth, but he can still enjoy the content.

Let's say that Mr. Kowalski was athletically accomplished in high school and college. He's now an octogenarian on a pain reliever and can't ambulate without a wheelchair. I wouldn't suggest that he sign up for an intramural football team, but maybe he could watch or even attend a game. Or maybe Mr. Kowalski was a poet or singer, still able to recall lyrics from his youth or willing to create new ones.

Psychiatric History

A history of mental-health issues, especially treatment with psychiatric medications, predisposes people to a greater risk of cognitive declines as they age. In general, psychiatric history includes past and present diagnoses (accurate or not) and treatments. Areas to investigate include a history of depression, anxiety, mood swings, thought disturbances, and substance use.

In addition to psychotropic medications, I ask about trauma, suicidal experiences, psychiatric hospitalization, electroconvulsive therapy (ECT), and individual, family, or relationship counseling. The biological and blended-family psychiatric histories might be relevant, especially regarding mood and thought disorders, dementia, suicide, and substance abuse.

Sometimes I revisit the patient's substance history from earlier in the evaluation to ensure that this significant, but often overlooked, factor gets the proper attention.

Physical Data

The cognitive evaluation involves more gathering of biopsychosocial data. Objective information includes a physical examination that addresses the patient as a whole, while scrutinizing individual systems. Documentation of hands-on assessments by family practitioners, internists, and other geriatric specialists is a vital supplement, along with laboratory findings and the data provided by nurses, social workers, nutritionists, pharmacists, speech and language pathologists, physical, occupational, and recreational therapists, geriatric-care managers, neuropsychologists, and the host of allied caregivers.

X-Rays and Blood

The pictures we can take of the brain and body from inside and out are nothing short of amazing, and often invaluable. Visualizing a problem substantiates what the clinician suspects or is unable to identify by an examination alone. Photography with microfibers, CT, and MRI scans of the brain and rest of the body can pinpoint locations of trauma or disease.

Specimens of blood, urine, and any removable solid or liquid also provide information about infections, inflammation, cancer, and other disorders of virtually any organ.

Laboratory tests are part of the dementia evaluation, because they help identify potential medical causes, especially those that can be corrected. Blood is checked for anemia, clotting, substances, and infection. Fluids, salts, kidney, thyroid, and liver functions are commonly assessed. Electroencephalograms, electrocardiograms, and x-rays verify brain, heart, and lung conditions. Again, only so many questions can be asked and tests run, so it's an algorithm of problem solving that determines the next evaluation decision.

A Neurologic Review

Motor and sensory functions are assessed by observing and testing for paralysis, balance, dexterity, and tremors while the patient is resting, and then performing activities. Speech, language, strength, reflexes, sensations, facial functions, taste, smell, and audio-visual abilities are also considered.

The Mental Status Exam

The mental-status exam is an objective evaluation of the patient's neuropsychiatric state at the moment. I document my observations while eliciting clinical performances and responses by the patient.

The following are some of the key parameters I review when assessing mood, thought, and cognitive function. The order in which the exam unfolds varies to accommodate the situation, and many of the questions simultaneously address a multitude of functions.

Appearance

Physical appearance, worth a thousand words, is our first clue to a patient's global health. Does he look well or not good at all? Alertness, facial expressions, skin integrity, difficulty breathing, and swollen ankles are some of the more immediate distress indicators that I observe for.

Is he happy, sad, anxious, or mad? Is he energized or comatose, cognitively present or seemingly demented? Is he obese, sickly thin or well nourished, groomed or disheveled?

Olfactory and audio input adds even more. Is she notably perfumed, smelling of urine or the sweet breath of diabetic ketoacidosis? Did I hear her moaning from pain or smacking her edentulous mouth due to thirst or nervous tick?

(Sometimes I walk into an extended-care facility and immediately notice the tired, disgruntled, food-stained faces and clothes of the people mulling about, and that's just the staff!)

Further assessment of appearance includes noticing posture, attire, and demeanor. Scalp and facial hair, makeup, body piercings, tattoos, skin lesions, tobacco-stained fingers and moustaches, scars, amputations, bandages, drainage tubes, oxygen masks, wheelchairs, and walkers are all visual cues.

While I certainly don't use my gustatory sense to taste patients, I do recognize and validate my gut reactions. As I have indicated in this book, there are nerve networks in our heads, hearts, and digestive systems, all of which are providing me with feedback.

The Pulse and the Tongue

Checking a patient's pulse provides a wealth of information that helps with diagnosis and treatment decisions. It's a credible medical assessment; especially useful for allowing me to appropriately touch someone who is sensory or cognitively impaired. It also promotes personal communication between the patient and caregiver. Sometimes it's my medical ticket for getting a patient to allow me to approach him or her at all.

In addition to the rate and rhythm, I sense the vitality. The pulse can feel abnormal from poor hydration, medications, emotional, cardiac, or other medical distress. A listless pulse isn't uncommon in people who suffer from vascular dementia, reflecting a tiring heart and hardening arteries.

While I'm listening to the patient's pulse, I can exam him more closely. I'm also listening and smelling.

When I'm in a patient's room or setting, I perform a visual sweep of the room contents and organization. I've seen the bag of candy on the diabetic's bedside table or the cigarette lighter of a smoker with oxygen-dependent lung disease, whose oxygen tubing is lying on the floor where someone will trip.

Checking the patient's pulse is a useful segue for "Please stick out your tongue." This quick clinical observation of an internal organ allows me to further assess the patient's attitude and neurologic ability to process the question and demonstrate a response. I've seen tongues so dry that medications were stuck on them.

Behavior

We demonstrate our intelligence by what we do and how we do it. Our actions and attitudes are reflected through aspects such as compliance, sociability, initiative, and judgment. Concern for others, manipulation, impulsivity, and drama are also among the varieties of behavior.

Patients are observed as acting happy, nervous, sad, angry, clear, or confused, depending on their cognitive state, their self-awareness, and whether their needs are being fulfilled. A patient's attitude might be cooperative, but she might be sluggish or uncoordinated. Restless behaviors driven by medical or psychological causes can manifest as pacing, rumination, or efforts to elope.

Declining motor coordination, failure to recognize objects, lack of understanding communications, and an inability to perform complex actions are behaviors consistent with moderate cognitive decline. Primitive mannerisms, seen in advancing dementia, include territoriality, food hoarding, and suspicion.

Orientation

Cognitively intact people are oriented to space and time. They know who and where they are, their age, the season, year, and general time of day. They understand their relationship to other people and their environment. A patient with delirium may or may not be oriented. Otherwise, failure to know these things means dementia is occurring—or you're on vacation.

It's not unreasonable for older adults to forget dates, especially if they have few scheduled activities or commitments. This is common among retired people who are without purpose or social networks. One day blurs into another.

It's a telling sign to meet patients in their homes or facilities who are watching news on television or reading the newspaper, yet cannot tell me the month, day, or year.

Becoming lost in time may be an act of preservation by repression, preferable to remembering insurmountable losses. Sometimes it's understandable that those with moderate-stage or worse dementia think it's twenty, forty, or sixty years earlier. They were happier back then.

Disorientation to location is a sign of moderate cognitive impairment, but that, too, needs to be regarded in context. I appreciate that some older patients have been relocated multiple times. Let's say that Mrs. Peterson's son, Peter, moves her across the country to be closer to his family. Mrs. Peterson, now in an unfamiliar city without her social contacts, falls and is hospitalized. She then goes to a rehabilitation hospital, and finally moves to a group-care home in another city, nearer her daughter Patti. Mrs. Peterson is understandably confused.

Not knowing one's own identity, however, reflects severe impairment, again due either to delirium or advanced cognitive declines. People who literally do not know themselves are approaching end-stage dementia.

Communication Skills

To communicate is to connect. Human communication occurs verbally and non-verbally, through motor gestures and body language. As a person's cognitions fail and sensory declines worsen, he loses the ability to sensibly stay in touch with the world around him. Dementia is a communications disconnect. I assess *how* a patient communicates as well as *what* is being communicated. I evaluate the physical ability to articulate speech, the logic of his language assembly, and the content of his narrative. I'm listening to his perceptions while assessing his neurological and psychological makeup.

Aphasic patients have lost the ability to receive, assemble, or express language. Sometimes that ability to communicate is compromised by a stroke, damaged cranial nerves, or drug toxicity.

Pain, ill-fitting dentures, dehydration, or panic can alter speech, as can social distress, anxiety, or anger. Medications often affect speech and language. Distorted nonsensical communications also occur with delirium or severe psychiatric distress.

Mood and Affect

The clinical assessment of mood is a subjective insight that originates in the patient, whose emotional state and cognitive acuities are interdependent. I simply ask, "How are you feeling?" or "How is your mood right now?" The answers determine if deeper scrutiny is warranted, including inquiries about self-harm or suicide. By observing his verbal and body language, thought processes, and attitude, I arrive at an objective judgment of the patient's mood and affect.

Affect refers to emotional expression. In addition to happy, sad, nervous, and mad, descriptors of affect include euphoria (excessive happiness), dysphoria (acute sadness), euthymia (stable calm emotion), and dysthymia (chronically depressed). Affect can be appropriate or inappropriate to context, consistent or inconsistent with mood, loose, or exaggerated and dramatized.

For example, Joe the Client is feeling down and bitter about getting older, but he keeps it to himself. He maintains a happy façade until one day he witnesses someone stumble and fall. Reacting to his own suppressed fears of pain and helplessness, Joe begins to simultaneously cry and laugh uncontrollably. Joe's behavior, driven by pent-up emotions, appears incongruent to his usual calm and compassionate demeanor his friends know him for.

This might be an appropriate time to ask Joe if he'd like to talk to someone about stress.

Insight

Insight is the awareness about, appreciation of, and point of view regarding one's own condition and circumstances. Healthy insight includes relating to the environment from one's own perspective as well as in relationship to others. Patients are constantly assessed for their insight to understand risks, benefits, and alternative treatments before they give consent for interventions that affect their life.

Sense and Insensibility

Our senses normally transmit information that we receive, organize, and interpret as thought, consciousness, memory, emotion, and other neurobiological expression. As elaborated in Chapter Two, sensorial deficits that cause or accompany cognitive declines are manifested as apraxia (loss of fine motor dexterity), agnosia (inability to recognize objects), aphasia (inability to manage words or language), amnesia (memory loss), and declines in taste, smell, touch, hearing, and vision.

The nature and consequences of sensorial decline depend on the location of the deficit. Mrs. Seymour's poor sense of vision, for example, may be due to compromises at various points along her nervous system. Cloudy lenses, detached retinas, optic-nerve tract or occipital lobe damage are all vulnerable regions to visual impairment.

Even if these areas are intact, sometimes the sensations can't be understood sensibly in the once-higher-functioning cerebral cortex regions of the brain. In this example, compromised vision and its misinterpretation could generate a sensation of great anxiety.

With aging, altered thoughts can coincide with certain cognitive and sensory disorders, relative to distinct brain-region involvement. In the elderly, the acute onset of altered sensations should always be considered a sign of a medical or medication problem, as opposed to a formal psychiatric derangement.

Common and Uncommon Sense

Thinking is an actively conscious experiencing of life. Thinking combines perception of the senses, dreams and imagination, emotions and ideas, awareness of the moment, and memories of the past and anticipation of the future. We employ our thoughts to recognize and solve intellectual, personal, and spiritual dilemmas. How, what, and why we think merge to create our understanding of mind awareness.

What does it mean to be of sound mind? Qualifiers include alertness, memory, and sensibility. To think clearly means to be able to register, process, and appreciate, functionally and logically, information as it's received in the brain. Healthy thinking is also linear—it's organized, coherent, and has a narrative flow. The following are descriptions of distorted thoughts that occur during delirium, dementia, and other cognitive impairments.

Circumstantial thought process is the term used to describe thinking that strays from or hedges around the central topic, using an excessive number of words to communicate very little information. An adage to describe circumstantial thinking is: "To make a short story long ..." However, the circumstantial talker ultimately returns to the original point.

Tangential thought process is similar: It branches off from a central topic. Unlike circumstantial, however, tangential thinkers tend not to return to the original point.

Disinhibited thought processes that often appear with dementia and delirium include ruminations or obsessions (incessant, nervous, thought dwellings) and suspicion (distrust). There is a lack of containment or loss of control against intrusive or inappropriate thoughts and feelings.

An *Idea of Reference* (IOR) is a distorted processing and misinterpretation of information that results in an irrational conclusion. The recipient incorrectly deciphers the information and adopts a special meaning. An example of IOR is someone viewing the Internet or television or listening to musical lyrics and thinking cryptic messages are being transmitted specifically and personally to him.

Flight of Ideas (FOI) refers to an erratic thought process. Likened to a game of pinball, the irregularity of the mind-flow is bizarre and seemingly random.

Hallucinations, Illusions, and Delusions

These are disturbances of logic and sensorial perception. Thought distortions occur because and as a consequence of medical or psychological imbalance. Impaired thinking can lead to losing touch with reality and manifest as poor judgment and inappropriate behavior.

A *hallucination* is a false sensorial experience that occurs in the absence of a physical stimulus outside the brain. The mind is triggering its own neurotransmitters to evoke the perception. Hallucinations take place solely in the imagination of the imaginer.

An olfactory (smell) hallucination can suggest a neurological problem, such as a seizure disorder. Tactile hallucinations are imagined movements of touch, such as bugs crawling or skin creeping, and are usually associated with delirium tremens of alcohol or another drug's side effects.

Visual or auditory hallucinations usually indicate a central-nervous-system disorder. These sensory distortions can occur in schizophrenia, dementia, delirium, substance intoxications, traumatic brain injury, and more.

Hallucinations can also occur from extreme sleep deprivation. People become psychotic (denial of reality) and start hallucinating as they approach 72 hours of absolute sleep deprivation.

An *illusion* is a misperception of an actual stimulus. While driving we might suddenly swerve to avoid hitting a small animal in the road, but the "animal" turns out to be a paper bag blowing across the pavement.

I see many patients (real ones and not in my imagination) who are diagnosed as having hallucinations, but are actually experiencing illusions. Their cognitive, visual, or hearing impairments cause much confusion: Shadows become people and background noises become gossip behind their backs (see "Sundowning"). Distorted senses often lead to paranoia.

A *delusion* is a belief system not commonly shared by others. In the year 1491, Christopher Columbus was regarded as delusional by most people, because he believed that the world was round. After 1492, those who still maintained that the world was flat were regarded as the delusional ones.

Paranoid delusions are unfounded fears of harm or persecution. Delusions of grandiosity are beliefs of special recognition or talent not founded in logic or sensibility.

The nature of the problem as expressed by the distressed patient (or informant) can provide significant information. As with any medical or psychiatric presentation, it's one thing to treat or suppress a delusion, but it's also important to interpret the root or theme of the perception's content.

For example, a woman with second-stage dementia once reported to me that while she slept at night, her husband and a female neighbor were having sex next to her in the same bed. Clinically, this qualified as paranoid (an unfounded fear of conspiracy) and delusional. I was able to validate her concern, but not her perception, and we agreed that our goal would include alleviating her stress. I subsequently learned that an infidelity had disrupted the marriage decades earlier. I also assessed that her medications and congested breathing were aggravating her insomnia.

Her erratic sleeping, waking, and surreal experiences reflected memories of the past confused with the present. Improving her sleep hygiene and regulating her medications reduced her paranoid delusions and distress.

Confabulation

Confabulation is giving false information, another common dementia behavior. It's a form of bluffing or lying in an effort to compensate for a cognitive deficit, such as poor memory or insight. The fabricator may not be aware of this behavior, depending on the degree of the intellectual deficit. Whether confabulation is done purposefully, the confabulator is attempting to maintain his or her integrity.

Judgment

Judgment is the ability to accurately understand information, make deliberate decisions, and behave appropriately. It vacillates during conditions such as acute stress, Sundowning, delirium, or intoxication, and disappears as dementia progresses. Judgment is a particularly scrutinized cognitive function of the dementia assessment, because it's often used for legal determination of a person's ability to independently manage his or her own life. Questions asked during the evaluation are meant to assess how people think and react to situations.

Hypothetical judgment includes knowing right from wrong, theoretically. Pragmatic judgment is actual behavior. For example, patients have acknowledged to me that it's risky and inappropriate to smoke cigarettes in bed or while wearing supplemental oxygen. That's sound judgment in the hypothetical sense. However, they then proceeded to smoke anyway, demonstrating poor pragmatic judgment.

Memory

The essence of dementia testing is: Don't forget to ask memory questions. Long- and short-term memory is demonstrated during the patient's subjective and medical-history recitation and formally, such as by asking him or her to deliberately remember three words and recalling them several minutes later. The evaluator also considers whether the patient is aware of or distressed by her own memory limits, is oblivious, or confabulates excuses.

Testing Cognition

Cognition is knowledge and the ability to learn and apply it deliberately and rationally. A patient's ability to perform complex intellectual functions attributed to the cerebral cortex is tested with questions that involve mathematics, grammar, and other intellectual acrobatics.

There is no shortage of clinical tests available to assist in diagnosing and monitoring cognitive disorders. Standardized testing utilizes formal terminology to facilitate communication among providers. These objective appraisals can validate the assessor's diagnosis. Examiner bias can't help but affect results, so testing promotes reliability.

Cognitive-function assessments range from simple question-and-answer interviews to extensive and invasive radiographic and chemical workups and analyses. Practitioners must realistically manage the time and expense involved with administering these tests.

Frequently used standardized tests include assessment of Activities of Daily Living (ADLs), Abnormal Involuntary Movement Scale (AIMS), and the Geriatric Depression Scale (GDS). Interviewer-assessment tests for assessing cognitive complexities also include the Clock Drawing Exam and the Folstein Mini-Mental Status Evaluation (MMSE).

The reader is referred to dementia reference texts or online for information about these and other available measures. What follows is a mental-status question that I developed as a quick, reliable, and inexpensive assessment of neurocognitive function.

The Four Coins

The Four Coins is a single question that samples many of the traditional measurements that usually necessitate multiple questions. I ask Mr. Winters to add together and tell me the total amount of a quarter, dime, nickel, and penny. On the surface it's a seemingly simple money and arithmetic problem, yet it offers profound insight into Mr. Winter's mental state.

Obviously, Mr. Winter's ability or inability to come up with the answer indicates his mental acuity. However, I also observe him for a universe of nuances during the process. I watch his mannerisms, his attitude, his ability to process the question, and his awareness for why we are engaging. Is he is pleasant, paranoid, anxious, or otherwise distressed? Does he realize why I'm asking this question and if he can answer it, or will he obsess, object, or bluff?

I ask my patients to calculate the Four Coins, because mental functions such as behavior, emotion, insight, abstraction, and higher-complexity intelligence are all assessed with this one question. The criteria for dementia, which involve memory, language, and visual-spatial dexterity, are addressed simultaneously. I use it to complement other cognitive tests and have discovered it to be of superior application for determining patients' abilities to function on their own.

Summing Up

The documents have been gathered and the lab and physical-exam results have been acquired. The patient has told his story and his mental status has been assessed. Medical problems and psychosocial stressors pertinent to the patient's condition have been evaluated.

It's time now to arrive at a diagnosis: a determination of dementia, delirium, or other cognitive deficit. The diagnostic profile also identifies mood issues, such as depression or PTSD, ambivalence, or suicidal ideations. Medical issues are acknowledged, along with thought and behavioral problems, such as paranoia, substance abuse, and personality disorders.

The evaluation ends with treatment recommendations. Medications may be started or stopped; more medical, neuropsychological, or occupational skill assessments may be requested; and resources contacted for case management, therapies, or living placements. An opinion might be rendered declaring whether the patient has the capacity to function independently or needs minimal or total care.

Thus, the root of practical treatment is to begin with a good assessment that leads to the correct diagnoses. To keep the weeds of life to a minimum, it's vital that practitioners, patients, and caregivers work together to keep communications clear and open.

In the next chapter I review pharmacology issues that are a prominent part of the cultural implications of dementia and its treatment.

Chapter Nine

MEDICATING DEMENTIA:
POLYGEROPSYCHOPHARMACOLOGY MADE SIMPLE

"He's the best physician that knows
the worthlessness of the most medicines."
—Benjamin Franklin

In this chapter I address medication issues relevant to cognition, mood, and behavior. I review their omnipresence in our lives and offer some guidelines for their use. I address some of the concerns for their overuse, especially among the senior population. I then look at the agents available for treatment and their risks and benefits. Some text may involve references to "off-label" medications originally approved for other reasons, but nevertheless used often.

I can share experiences, opinions, and suggestions. I cannot, however, give treatment advice. This I *can* tell you: Repeated exposure to psychoactive drugs increases the potential to permanently alter the life course of any individual's mind and body.

Psychotropics and World History

A drug is an ingested substance that has no nutritional value, but evokes a physical response. "Psychotropic" generally refers to a drug that evokes a central-nervous-system response. "Psychoactive" refers to any stimulus that causes a mind response.

Psychotropics exist in nature and people have always used them. Alcohol, opium, coca, marijuana, tobacco, and hallucinogens have been used for thousands of years. Like never before, they're now synthesized, manufactured, and marketed for medical, spiritual and recreational purposes.

We've mastered the ability to synthesize our well-being. Yet physical exercise, intellectual stimulation, and proper nutrition will always be the fundamental building blocks for a healthy psychoactive life. Pharmaceuticals are a life-saving and life-enhancing benefit to longevity in modern times, which has undoubtedly evolved thanks to advances in medications. We need, however, to maintain a realistic balance between artificial and natural, and appropriate versus harmful.

Everything Is Psychoactive

Technically, any stimulus that evokes nerve activity is psychoactive. Sight, sound, taste, smell, and touch can all induce a psychoactive response. Memories and dreams also have psychoactive qualities; they're physical byproducts of chemical interactions occurring in the nervous system.

Virtually all pharmaceuticals have a psychoactive capacity. The mere thought of using a medicine can have psychological implications. Drugs that target other body functions likely also affect the nervous system. It's the rare medication meant for heart, lung, liver, or any other function that doesn't affect the brain.

As humans have always activated and sedated themselves with substances, medicinally and recreationally, it's not uncommon for some to use mind-altering drugs daily and continuously. The less potent stimulants in common use are caffeine and nicotine. The most common sedative is alcohol. The effects of even these psycho-active agents can be cumulative and conflicting. Their potencies are magnified when combined.

I'm a physician who shares the growing concern about overuse of psychiatric drugs, and not just in the elderly. For example, a precarious development that has become standard practice is the use of powerful mind-altering medications for everyday issues. The Food and Drug Administration (vulnerable to industry influence) has approved several antipsychotic medications for the treatment of depression or mood swings. A similar danger has now been realized with antibiotics like penicillin: Excessive and nonchalant use has resulted in illness resistance. You may feel better today, but the effect will be temporary and the side effects years from now can be catastrophic.

In the medical setting, it seems to me that too many physicians and other providers are losing the art of judicious diagnosing and prescribing and are consequently overmedicating their patients. This is also due to the demands and expectations of so many patients and families who feel they must receive medications at a hospital or doctor's visit.

To reverse the trend of polygeropsychopharmacology and recapture practicality requires objective education. Pharmacological knowledge includes how medications work, their expected outcomes, and side-effect profiles. This is basic pharmacology.

Biochemistry, physics, anatomy, and a little astrology are key disciplines for understanding medication management.

Psychoactive Prevalence

We live in a chemical world. In our everyday lives, whether or not we take prescription medications, we're exposed to the artificial manipulation of our senses, minds, and thus our bodies.

Air fresheners, soaps, and cleaning products permeate our indoor environments. Hygiene products are chemically enhanced to be pleasing to our senses. Many of the beverages and foods we consume are chemically enhanced for flavor and energy.

Pharmacologic Guidelines

Mr. Pillman starts his day when the nurse brings him his medications in a two-ounce paper cup, along with two ounces of water. He swallows a thyroid pill, codeine for pain, two cognitive enhancers, a stool softener, three blood-pressure pills, an anti-cholesterol drug, an appetite-promoting anti-depressant, and a muscle relaxant.

I once evaluated a 76-year-old woman brought to my office by a transport driver with no information other than a bag of medications. In addition to vitamin supplements, I found 15 different prescription bottles, empty and filled. Eleven had direct neuropsychiatric effects. There were eight different prescribing physicians.

Pharmacologic management of dementia and related issues is the focus of this chapter, so it's pertinent to preview prescribing guidelines here.

Free Samples Are Costly

The epidemic of free drug sampling by pharmaceutical companies through doctors' offices continues to flourish. The following are some truths you need to know in regards to so-called complimentary medications you may be receiving for treatment of mood, memory, and sleep.

Medications aren't candy. Drug companies invest a lot of money persuading doctors to distribute the goods. Pretty packaging and clever advertising campaigns are luring not just unsuspecting consumers, but even worse, doctors and nurses who rely solely on the drug industry for education about the medicines. Some practitioners may deny this, but it's becoming difficult to obtain objective information. The drug companies that stand to gain financially underwrite many research and professional journals. A lot of organized health conferences continue to rely on drug-company-sponsored lectures, entertainment, and meals.

Free-sample medications are more potent than ever before. No one single new psychiatric drug on the market doesn't already exist either in a generic or less powerful variation. People may be feeling better on the new drugs because they're stronger, and therefore more likely to create dependence. The argument that the new generation of antipsychotic, anti-depressant, or sleep-promoting medication is unique or has less side effects is a manipulation of the truth.

Free samples are EXPENSIVE! Wait until you discover that your insurance won't authorize the new medication and your doctor has no more samples. Hundreds of millions of dollars are budgeted by government each year for these drugs, influenced by lobbied laws that prevent negotiations based on pricing. Every dollar spent in the public and private sectors on these unnecessarily expensive non-exceptional drugs means a dollar less for personnel, facility, and welfare services that could help hundreds of thousands of seniors.

Rule of Least Restriction, Redux

Least restrictive medication management respects the chemical risks unique to seniors' physiologies compared to younger adults. Other aging vulnerabilities such as ill health, poor nutrition, other medications and side effects, resource accessibility, and financial and emotional costs need to be considered when deciding proper dosages.

Drug-Drug Interactions

A general rule for prescription medication is that taking four pharmaceuticals carries a fifty percent likelihood of having some type of drug-to-drug interaction. The odds of this occurring are almost certain with six or more agents in the body.

Treatment Versus Masking

"Masking" refers to a superficial resolution of a problem without correcting the underlying cause. Drug therapy may suppress a symptom, but it can risk worsening the original problem or causing new ones.

As seen in the section on dandelion medicine, good pharmaceutical management includes addressing the root of an illness. It's not enough to treat chest pain with numbing medications without evaluating for an underlying emergency such as a heart attack. A cough suppressant might provide temporary comfort, but a confirmation of pneumonia necessitates invasive medication treatment. Knowing why a person isn't sleeping well may be more vital than which sleeping pill to prescribe. I wouldn't want to induce sleep by causing a respiratory arrest.

The agitation of delirium can be appropriately treated with psychiatric sedatives. It can be risky, however, not to pursue and correct the instigation, for example, a bladder, prostate, or sinus infection, or a hidden substance-abuse withdrawal. Until the original problem is discovered and corrected, side effects of medications, such as dehydration and constipation, falling, and reduced blood perfusion to the brain, can cause the patient to become even more perturbed than before treatment.

Acute Versus Chronic Interventions

Sometimes, short-term solutions result in long-term problems. Medications useful for acute interventions are often, and unfortunately, continued indefinitely, even after the medical issue is repaired. Or a patient is discharged from a brief hospitalization with a prescription for six months of sleeping pills.

Crutches and Braces

A medication is sometimes a "crutch," used for appropriate short-term stability, until the partaker can figuratively stand on his or her own two feet again. Other times, medications may be indefinitely vital and act like a permanent "brace," giving security and function. The policy of "doing no harm" means that caution and monitoring are needed in both cases to prevent unnecessary chemical dependency or delayed physical, neurological, and cognitive adversities.

Prior To Admission (PTA)

Prior to Admission is a medical reference to awareness of a patient's behaviors preceding a clinical encounter. Knowing a person's medical and social history greatly supplements the evaluation of the picture before your eyes.

I repeat this because it's so incredibly common: Frequently

overlooked is the substance history prior to the person becoming a patient. Remote or current use of alcohol is a prevalent contributor to many dementias; so are other prescription and over-the-counter stimulants and sedatives, cigarettes, caffeine, laxatives, pain medicines, sinus and allergy drugs, heart pills, and basically anything else that's ingestible.

I once treated a young adult whose erratic thoughts, moods, and behavior turned out to be a result of his PTA dependence on an over-the-counter cough medicine containing alcohol and antihistamine. I've also been in homes of elderly clients (by invitation, of course) and discovered their heart, lung, and pain prescriptions, over-the counter sleeping pills, and muscle relaxants. Sometimes the bottles are full, sometimes empty, and sometimes mixed. Who knew?

Cross-Coverage

If it's not known that a patient might be withdrawing from any kind of substance, then the insomnia, anxiety, or psychosis that occurs might be misdiagnosed and mistreated.

Alcohol and prescribed tranquilizers often substitute or "cross-cover" for each other. Withdrawal from substance use and misuse doesn't always present itself during the time of acute medical or psychiatric intervention. I've seen the effects postponed for weeks in patients who don't develop delirium until after being released from the hospital to a long-term-care facility. Their substance-dependence problem prior to hospitalization hadn't been realized while they received analgesics, sleeping pills, and muscle relaxants that delayed any withdrawal until discontinued coincident with the transfer.

Therapeutic Levels

Certain medications can be monitored for safety and efficacy by measuring their levels in the blood. Some medicines for heart, blood, thyroid, and neurologic and psychiatric conditions, for example, have clinically accepted blood levels. These laboratory values are used as guidelines for treating the whole person.

There are no established therapeutic blood levels, however, for the geriatric population. Metabolism slows down with aging, even more so from years of medication exposures. So-called "normal" measured blood levels of drugs, such as lithium, phenytoin (Dilantin), or digitalis, can be extremely toxic in an elderly or medically compromised person.

I try to avoid high-dosage prescribing anyway, so elevated levels for my patients are rarely a problem. If levels do get too high, another medical imbalance, such as dehydration or an infection, is usually occurring that explains the level change.

Medications Have Delayed Effects

Some medications take effect immediately, which is critical for treating heart attacks, strokes, and behavior emergencies. Stimulants elevate blood pressure, rapidly or insidiously. Tranquilizers can quickly avert violence or gradually dull the senses.

With continuous use, however, there is tolerance. Psychoactive substances alter metabolic activity. Natural neurotransmitters adjust to the introduction of synthetic neurotransmitters. A new symbiosis, an alliance and reliance, is created between the body and the medication. Higher doses are required to elicit the desired effect, creating psychological and physiological dependence.

Sedatives, such as those used for pain, sleep, and anxiety, help us feel better, but can accumulate in the body. Rebound restlessness and outright aggression occur when the sedative actions wear off. This leads to an increased use of sedatives in a vicious cycle. Impaired energy and focus, memory loss, and blackouts (such as sleep-eating at night) worsen over time. Declines in judgment and medical health ensue, increasing toxicity risks. The stage is set for falling and breaking a hip, being misdiagnosed with dementia, or actually developing it unnecessarily.

Conversely, stimulants activate the body, elevating energy and mood. Side effects, delayed or sometimes immediate, are consistent with body over-activation; headaches, digestive problems, sleep interference, and increased anxiety are common. High blood pressure and other vascular diseases develop. Parkinsonism, a form of chemically induced Parkinson's disease, is also a risk of chronic psycho-stimulant use that might not become evident for years.

Psychotropics and Neurotransmitters

Neurotransmitters are chemicals that transport electrical energy from nerve to nerve, and synapse gap to gap. Neurotransmitters are found throughout the brain, spinal cord, and peripheral and autonomic nerves that cover every inch of the body, to the smallest neurological branch. Every organ system and metabolic function is neurologically involved. We are all, indeed, a bundle of nerves.

Psychotropics may be intended for a specific mental outcome, but they *all* affect other neurotransmitters to various degrees and have a significant impact both within and outside the central nervous system. When any person, young or old, takes a drug, he alters not just moods, thoughts, and behaviors. Heart, lungs, kidneys, endocrine glands, blood cells, bones, and digestive and every other system do not escape the parts-per-millions presence of modern chemistry.

Our heart's nervous system is independent and interdependent with the central nervous system. So is our stomach, which has been referred to as an "enteric brain." We refer to our intestinal "gut feelings" for good reason; the digestive system, the nearby adrenal glands, and the central nervous system possess abundantly similar neurotransmitters.

Therefore, when we recognize and validate the feelings and thoughts of our head, heart, and stomach, the experience is legitimate. Perhaps this best describes intuition.

Clinically significant, as mentioned earlier, is that when psychotropic medications affect brain neurotransmitters, they also influence the heart and digestive systems.

Neurotransmitters, Medications, and You

Neurotransmitters found in the central nervous system (and elsewhere bodily) include dopamine, serotonin, norepinephrine, gamma aminobutyric acid (GABA), glutamate, and acetylcholine. These compounds regulate brain activity, such as memory, cognition, breathing, sleeping, laughter, and fear. These neurotransmitters are the focus of action of most neurologic and psychiatric medications. They're also subject to the side effects of many other medications unintended for the nervous system.

Uppers and Downers

Pharmaceutical activity falls into two categories: stimulants and suppressants. Regardless of the drug and the body system targeted, a pharmaceutical agent does one of two things: It either speeds or slows physiologic activity.

Sometimes drugs excite a neurotransmitter activity, resulting in a paradoxically suppressed body function. An example is stimulating the release of endorphins that blunt pain. Conversely, suppression may be the mechanism for stimulating an action. A drug that reduces anxiety might allow someone to proceed with an engaging activity.

Psychostimulant medications are used to treat depression, inattentiveness, and energy deficiencies by activating metabolism. Their side effects include restlessness, insomnia, and erratic blood pressure. Sedatives calm central-nervous-system anxieties, but also slow autonomic and peripheral nerve functions that can inhibit heartbeat and respiration and dull mental functions.

Most of us naturally seek alertness in the daylight hours. Socially accepted stimulants readily available include coffee in the morning and other caffeinated beverages during the day. As evening approaches, biological activity levels tend to decrease. Nighttime behavior is usually more relaxed and calm, a time for sedatives to enhance the evening.

Sedatives can initially activate the consumer. Chemical activity in the brain is suppressed, allowing euphoria and impulsive expressions of otherwise inhibited thoughts and behaviors. Later, there is depression.

Diphenhydramine is an example of an exceptionally popular over-the-counter drug with mixed effects. It's the active ingredient in Benadryl, many cold and allergy agents, and the "PM" component of nighttime medications. Frequently, it initially sedates, but then causes concurrent restlessness.

A Third Category

Actually, a third category of pharmaceutical activity combines both a stimulant and suppressant in one compound.

Mixing uppers and downers is nothing new; humans have

forever been taking them together. It's quite prevalent in many cultures. Many people enjoy alcohol in their coffee. Alcohol mixed with caffeine-fortified energy drinks has become especially popular in recent years. Sinus and head-cold preparations often have both active and suppressive ingredients. Somewhere in this world someone is blending a combination of natural coca and opium. Elsewhere, especially in America, someone is ingesting an amphetamine along with a tranquilizer, as prescribed.

Combination formulations can be beneficial in the treatment of heart, respiratory, and many other illnesses and infections. Their side effects, however, can confuse other functions.

Seniors who take a lot of drugs usually expose themselves to the conflicting effects of uppers and downers. I frequently encounter patients whose medications include a thyroid stimulant, an activating breathing steroid, urination-stimulating diuretics, another that stimulates urinary retention, pain relievers, muscle relaxants, and an anxiety suppressant. Further complicating the profile is the challenge of taking the correct medicines in the correct dosages at the correct times with the correct foods.

The tolerance that an elderly user might develop to chronic medication exposure is offset by his increased nerve-receptor sensitivities. Thus, I cannot overemphasize that elderly patients' pharmacology situations are vastly different than that of young and middle-aged adults.

Psychiatric Drugs for Dementia Management

Psychotropic medications activate or suppress brain chemistry by altering neurotransmitter production, receptor activity and metabolic breakdown. The following are conventional medicine drugs frequently prescribed (as seen in Chapter Four), based on their proposed chemical target.

Serotonin has a calming effect and is one of the leading neurotransmitters attributed to mood. Its deficiency has been associated with depression and suicide; accordingly, many antidepressants are serotonin-promoting. When beneficial, this category of medication stabilizes depression, in part due to an anti-anxiety action. Since serotonin receptors are also abundant in the gastrointestinal tract, the brain may feel more tranquil, but the stomach is nauseous. Too much serotonin gives us headaches and muscle and stomach cramps, not unlike influenza symptoms.

Serotonin medications include: amitriptylin (Elavil), imipramine (Tofranil), sertraline (Zoloft), paroxetine (Paxil), escitalopram (Lexapro), and fluoxetine (Prozac).

Norepinephrine (NE) is an activating neurotransmitter created as a by-product of dopamine; it's also a synthesized drug. Illicit and prescription amphetamine drugs stimulate this nerve chemical and its activity, along with dopamine. These adrenaline-like activating drugs promote mood, energy, attentiveness, and motivation, and are often used in conjunction with physical rehabilitation therapies.

One side effect, appetite loss, makes this category of medication sought after for weight reduction, but this is usually not a healthy strategy. Even at small doses, it can adversely stimulate heart rate and blood pressure or cause anxiety and insomnia.

Norepinephrine-promoting prescription medications include bupropion (Wellbutrin), atomoxetine (Strattera), methylphenidate

(Ritalin, Concerta), modafinil (Provigil), and amphetamine/dextro-amphetamine (Adderall).

As I've indicated, medications usually have multiple effects on multiple receptors, but several popular anti-depressants have deliberate multiple neurotransmitter activities, affecting both serotonin and norepinephrine, such as venlafaxine (Effexor) and duloxetine (Cymbalta).

GABA (gamma-amino-butyric acid) is a neurotransmitter involved in regulating the readiness of nerve cells to fire. GABA deficiency is related to seizures, mood swings, impulsivity, and aggressive behaviors. GABA-promoting agents are often very effective for treating these problems and in managing some dementias.

GABA medications include valproic acid/divalproex (Depakote), carbamazepine (Tegretol), gabapentin (Neurontin), tiagabine (Gabitril), and pregabalin (Lyrica). Potential side effects include sedation or metabolic disruptions.

Benzodiazepine drugs are closely related to GABA's neurotransmitters and receptors. This popular sedative class includes such favorites as diazepam (Valium), alprazolam (Xanax), lorazepam (Ativan), clonazepam (Klonopin), triazolam (Halcion), and temazepam (Restoril).

As mentioned in the chapter on sleep and dementia, some newer sleeping medications are GABA-oriented, such as zolpidim (Ambien), eszoplicone (Lunesta), and zaleplon (Sonata), but they occupy the benzodiazepine receptor site and need to be treated with the same cautions as traditional sleeping pills. Their effectiveness for calming can be offset by confusion, falls, and paradoxical irritability.

Dopamine (DA) is involved in regulating motor movement. Its depletion is linked to Parkinson's disease, tremors, rigidity, mental dullness, and dementia. Medications that replenish dopamine are used to treat Parkinson's and related body-movement abnormalities (tremor, imbalance, and rigidity), and for calming restless leg syndrome.

Dopamine-promoting prescription drugs include carbidopa/ levodopa (Sinemet), ropinirole (Requip), and pramipexole (Mirapex).

Dopamine also induces euphoria and hallucinations. Substances such as cocaine and amphetamines create pleasurable feelings, but the downside is dopamine diminution with subsequent insomnia, aggression, or psychosis.

I frequently encounter patients mentally confused from simultaneously receiving both DA-promoting and -blocking agents.

Dopamine-blocking agents, known as antipsychotics, neuroleptics, and major tranquilizers, are given to stop hallucinations and agitation in people with delirium or schizophrenic psychosis. The side effects are Parkinson's-like: severe stiffness, difficulty swallowing, trembling, and restless thoughts. Dopamine-blocking agents that have been on the market for many years include haloperidol (Haldol), chlorpromazine (Thorazine), perphenazine (Trilafon), and thiothixene (Navane).

Antipsychotic medications given alone can cause mental frustration, abnormal motor movements and restlessness, or make swallowing difficult. Benzodiazepines help offset many of the side effects of antipsychotics. Dispensed together, they often allow use of lower total dosages because of their complementary actions.

When appropriately administered for the right reasons, the combination of benzodiazepines and antipsychotic medications is often an effective and beneficial pharmaceutical approach for management of delirium and agitated dementia.

Newer drugs in this category include clozapine (Clozaril), risperidone (Risperdal), olanzepine (Zyprexa), quetiapine (Seroquel), ziprasidone (Geodon), and aripiprazole (Abilify). (Don't you love the names?)

These recent-to-market drugs are being touted as uniquely effective and absent of traditional side effects. Scientific support for the claims, however, has not held well and, in my clinical experience and opinion, the newer drugs have as many, if not more, side effects and are superior only in price.

Glutamate is an activating neurotransmitter that has been implicated as a culprit in memory and cognitive decline. The theory behind pharmacologically suppressing glutamate activity is that it will reduce over-stimulation and thus delay nerve cell fatigue and death, thereby preserving memory and other mental function.

Memantine (Namenda) is presently marketed for management of Alzheimer's Dementia. Whether there's benefit from this medication is controversial, but occurrences of nausea and mental restlessness are real.

Acetylcholine is one of the neurotransmitters foremost associated with learning and memory. Acetylcholine-depleted neurons are considered a leading correlate of Alzheimer's and related cognitive declines.

Two of the most marketed acetylcholine-promoting prescription medications are donepezil (Aricept) and rivastigmine (Exelon). Pharmaceutically stimulated acetylcholine activity theoretically stalls faltering intellect, thus preserving the individual's living independence. There have also been allegations of behavior-calming effects from cognitive enhancing medications. The validity of these claims remains very equivocal.

Acetylcholine-promoting medications have side effects throughout the body, especially the gastrointestinal tract. They frequently cause stomach upset, excessive salivation, and loose bowels. Headaches, significant irritability, and insomnia are other common adversities.

In contrast are the acetycholine-blocking medications that, as I also mentioned above (diphenhydramine) and in Chapter Four, are used daily by millions of people around the world. They help by reducing inflammation and suppressing metabolic over-reactivity. Their side effects work opposite of the enhancing drugs, causing constipation, urine retention, and dehydration, but also paradoxical irritability and insomnia.

Many psychiatric medications have this pharmacologic side effect that can at times be used to advantage. Too often, however, they are prescribed with a limited regard for their adverse potential. Anticholinergic delirium is a term applied to psychosis induced by these kinds of drugs.

Pharmacology of Alzheimer's

Presently, donepezil (Aricept), galantamine (Reminyl), rivastigmine (Exelon), and tacrine (Cognex), along with memantine (Namenda) are officially approved by the Food and Drug Agency for Alzheimer's Dementia in its various stages.

Pending developments in pharmacologic treatment of Alzheimer's include genetically interrupting the abnormal protein formation and deposition of neurofibrillary tangles and amyloid plaques. These attacks on the disease at its molecular roots might prove effective, but potential side effects and interactions with other drugs will determine feasibility.

Do the current medications work? The answer, like the dementia experience itself, is ambiguous. Current information about cognitive enhancers is subject to dispute. The pharmaceutical companies control much of the data, so objective conclusions are hard to come by. Also, as we've seen, the effectiveness of any medication is dependent on many factors.

Considering all the mitigating aspects and my own years of clinical practice, my answer has to be this: Sometimes cognitive enhancers help, but usually they don't. Sometimes they offer hope and often they make behaviors worse. And they cost a lot of money.

In short, I haven't seen much benefit. Maybe it's because most patients I treat are on multiple medications and have several medical problems. Surprisingly common is the number of patients who are on multiple drugs whose pharmacological activities work exactly opposite each other!

Usually, when I taper the cognition-related drugs (and a few other psychoactive medications), patients become less restless. I consider it progress when a patient shows no adverse response to a reduction in medication; the person is the same on less chemicals.

So, How Do I Prescribe?

I start thinking about it while I'm conducting the assessment. I'm evaluating a person and a biological system, living in context to his or her environment. I try to understand the *roots* and medical realities of each patient's physical, psychological, and social profile.

I avoid adding more medications and I try to substitute or reduce them when I think they're unnecessary. Sometimes I make no changes, because doing so creates the risk of upsetting their fragile metabolic balance. If I'm consulted on a patient and discover he's on twenty-five different prescription drugs, it's time to weed the garden, gently.

My choice and dosage of agents depend on what mood, thought, or behavior I'm trying to enhance or suppress. I assess the medical, medication, and life-situational profile of the person and decide if prescribing more agents will truly cause an overall benefit.

I regard drug strength and duration, costs, and availability. I start with conservative doses and perhaps most importantly, I *always* consider their side-effect profiles and drug-drug interactions. Also, I *always* prefer non-pharmacologic interventions.

Managing diseases and their symptoms pharmacologically is an intrusion on nature. If I can't help, I try to do no harm. However, when a medication intervention does improve a person's quality of life, the response is gratifying to the patient, the provider, and everyone else.

Chapter Summary

As I've emphasized throughout this chapter, we expose ourselves to a lot of chemicals that have the capacity to provide benefit or cause harm. Just because a medication is FDA approved, available with or without a prescription, or advertised as effective does not guarantee safety.

The cost of a drug isn't just what you pay at the pharmacy. Additional costs include office visits, laboratory monitoring, insurance premiums and telephone calls, and, as always, the expense to our physical, neurocognitive, and emotional balance.

A medication's effectiveness is determined by the person who takes it. Breathing medications can't really offset cigarette smoking.

Insulin can go only so far against improper nutrition. Consuming caffeine in the evening counteracts sleeping pills. Antidepressants are limited against sedatives and polypharmacy. Pure and simple: Don't expect medications to work unless your behaviors encourage them to.

Every person's health profile is different and every prescribing situation is unique. Still, knowledge and common sense play an important role. Practitioners, caregivers, and patients share responsibility for communications and decision-making. It's not enough to rely on the media or the pharmaceutical industry as primary resources of information. It's important to learn about health care and other chemical products from non-biased authoritative sources. Be involved with your own medical care by being informed. Ask questions. Knowledge is empowerment for living longer and better, with and without pharmaceuticals.

The best "medicine," of course, is staying healthy physically, nutritionally, and mentally so that medications aren't needed. Next best is to require the least amount of medication necessary.

You might need to participate in your own health disciplines if you want to enjoy the aging process. Your body will thank you. So will your mind, your wallet, your spouse, your friends and family, the Earth, and the universe.

Ten Clinical Suggestions
For the Geriatric Caregiver

1. *Maintain Integrity.* A dementia patient with child-like behaviors can still be managed with dignity. Practitioner integrity is maintained by acting neither superior nor submissive.

2. *Rule of Least Restriction.* Medications, along with physical and environmental interventions, need to cause as little disruption and restraint as is feasible.

3. *Therapeutic Levels Aren't Always.* What may be regarded as subtherapeutic medicating for a young adult could be toxic to an elderly person.

4. *Four Is A Lot, Six Is A Lot More.* Older adults are vulnerable to taking a lot of medications. Drug-drug interactions become very prominent by the half-dozen mark.

5. *The Four Coins.* Ask the person to add together a quarter, dime, nickel, and penny. If he or she cannot do so correctly, chances are he is unable to independently manage medical or daily living needs.

6. *Think Medical.* Consider acute mental changes in the elderly as symptoms of an underlying medical derangement. If no medical etiology exists, then consider psychosocial factors (e.g., losses).

7. *B & B.* No, this doesn't stand for Bed & Breakfast. Bowel and bladder problems are leading causes of erratic mentation or behavior in the elderly. Insufficient fluid intake and medication side effects (e.g., diuretics, sedatives, anti-cholinergics) are common instigators.

8. *Alcohol.* A covert problem for any age group, when it comes to alcohol, elderly clients sometimes can't, or won't, share information about consumption which can be vital for correct diagnosis and treatment.

9. *Ambivalence Is Not Suicide.* Indifference or the desire not to live needs to be differentiated from wanting to kill oneself, and should be approached accordingly.

10. *Feel The Pulse.* Don't just check rhythm and count rate. *Feel* it, hear it with your touch; listen to the vitality of the person behind the heartbeat.

EPILOGUE

ABSCISSION

"Don't go—not yet—not yet—but
the day slipped away as fast as any other."
—Margaret Craven

Abscission is the process of trees detaching themselves from their leaves. Triggered by the seasonal lengthening of nighttime hours and dropping temperatures, hormonal shifts cause swelling of the tubules at the junction of the branch and the leaf stem. Circulation is choked off and the leaf, losing its ability to metabolize the sunlight, air, water, and nutrients that once flowed through its veins, dies.

Abscission marks the beginning of autumn. Soon, the tree will rest and the leaves will perform their colorful last living acts. Leaves fall, having left behind next spring's buds.

There Was Evening and There Was Morning, One Day

From fertilization until death, life is a constant succession of moments that begin and end. Somewhere in the world the sun is setting, while elsewhere it is rising.

As we sprout through youth, we learn that all things must pass. We say goodbye to childhood and hello to adolescence. Reaching into adulthood, we branch out into the world and stake our place under the sun, for however many seasons fortune affords us.

Gerolescence prepares us for abscission. It is the death of one form of productive years and the birth of another. It is (are you ready for this?) the *springtime of the autumn* of new passions, experiences, and brilliant colors.

Healthy gerolescents are the communicators of wisdom to be passed on to future generations. Septuagenarians, octogenarians, and beyond have known spring rains, summer sunrises, autumn leaves, and winter sunsets. They have buried loved ones, said goodbye to pets, places, and people, and greeted their newborn grandchildren and great-grandchildren with a kiss.

They have seen and listened, tasted and smelled, and touched. Such is the beauty of getting older. You learn to savor moments.

And you shall be like a tree planted by streams of water,
That bringeth forth its fruit in its season,
And whose leaf doth not wither.
—Psalms 1:3

INDEX

ACKNOWLEDGMENTS

This book is made possible by the collective efforts of many who encouraged me in creating this work. I hope my words have been helpful and stimulated a few thoughts worth pondering. If so, then I am grateful.

On this beautiful winter day I want to thank and acknowledge my wonderful wife, children, parents and siblings, and all the branches of the family tree. To friends and neighbors like Ron, Mike, and Jim. To my patients, co-workers, colleagues and teachers for being teachers.

Thanks to Health ED for taking a chance on me. To personal and business mentors recently in my life such as Larry Hughes and Byron Green, and to the many others who I already have or will meet on the path that is my destiny.

A special thank you to my editor and friend, Deke Castleman, for accepting the job of coach.

December 20, 2008
Lizard Camp
Portola, CA

ABOUT THE AUTHOR

STEVEN E. RUBIN, M.D., is an American Board of Psychiatry and Neurology-certified Adult Psychiatrist specializing in Geriatric Psychiatry, currently in private practice in Reno, Nevada.

He received his medical degree from Southern Illinois University School of Medicine, completed his internship at Duke University, and graduated from residency at the University of Virginia.

He is a Clinical Associate Professor with the University of Nevada-Reno School of Medicine and a member of the Nevada Medicaid Drug Utilization Review Board.

Dr. Rubin gives workshops and lectures on geriatric care to various health and civic groups across the nation. His professional mission is to deliver quality health care and education to gerolescent adults, their families, and the community.

Please visit his website at www.Gerolescence.com for information regarding copies of this book or speaking engagements.